AF711318

ORCHIDS

ORCHIDS

Text by J. Oplt

Illustrations by J. Kaplická

SPRING BOOKS

Translated by Joy Turner-Kadečková
Designed and produced by Artia for Spring Books

Published by
The Hamlyn Publishing Group Limited
LONDON • NEW YORK • SYDNEY • TORONTO
Hamlyn House, Feltham, Middlesex, England

© copyright ARTIA 1970
Reprinted 1972

ISBN 0 600 02883 6

Printed in Czechoslovakia by Svoboda
3/01/02/51

CONTENTS

Introduction	7
Orchidaceae	9
The Blossoms and Fruits of Orchids	11
Conditions for Growth	12
Care of Orchids Imported from the Tropics	16
Soil	17
Flowerpots and Baskets	18
Transplanting Orchids	18
Feeding Orchids	20
Harmful Insects and Diseases	21
Propagation of Orchids	22
Plates	27
Index	140

Introduction

When Europeans discovered their first orchid at the opening of the 16th century, hundreds of enthusiasts set out for the most remote corners of the world to search for other new species. They made expeditions to the virgin forests of Brazil, to the dark jungles of Borneo, they cut their way through the overgrown banks of rivers in India and Asia Minor and penetrated as far as the mountains of Madagascar. Every new discovery was the result of superhuman effort, courage and self-denial. It is hard to say whether each expedition represented a hunt for fairy-tale treasures, or the passion which characterizes every hunter.

The first orchid was brought to Europe by the Spaniards in 1510. This was the *Vanilla* which, after the Saffron Crocus, provided the most expensive flavouring extract. It was not until a century later however, in 1635, that a really decorative orchid was imported, namely the North American *Cypripedium reginae*. In 1641 it appeared on the list of plants cultivated at the Botanical Garden at Leyden. Until 1800 orchids were very rare and even the most valuable floral collections of Europe at that time could boast only a few samples. The Berlin Botanical Garden resembled the Paris Botanical Garden by having only seven species of exotic orchid in 1804. The Schönbrunn in Vienna cultivated eleven species of orchid while Leyden had only three species. The reason for this was that thousands of imported orchids died during their journey from exotic lands, or later on in greenhouses, as a result of the lack of knowledge of conditions in which orchids lived and thrived. It was not until 1845 when Belgian collector Jean Linden travelled in South and Central America, that more accurate reports on the conditions in which tropical orchids thrived became available.

Even at that time certain enterprising horticulturists endeavoured to encourage wholesale trade in orchids. However, the heavy losses experienced during importation of these rare plants discouraged quite a number. The four largest and most flourishing enterprises in Britain were Sander, Veitch, Low and Charlesworth, in Belgium van Houtte, and in France Morell. The most successful of them all was, and continued to be for many years, Sander of Britain.

The plants imported into Europe usually had seed capsules which often scattered ripe seeds on the roots of the orchids en route. It was thus at the beginning of the nineteenth century that Dr. Salisbury began to observe the germination of seeds on imported plants. In the greenhouses of a horticultural firm at Chiswick seeds of the species *Prescottia plantaginea* germinated on the walls of flowerpots. The first attempts to cross orchids were made by the head gardener of the firm Veitch in London, a certain John Dominy, in 1853. In 1856 he cultivated his first hybrids of the family *Calanthe*, followed later by others.

The age of big orchid hunters is over. Today reliable methods of large-scale orchid cultivation are known. New varieties and species unknown to even the densest virgin forests have been cultivated in greenhouses. Specialized horticultural establishments all over the world cultivate hundreds of thousands in the most varied colour combinations. We find them among other house plants in homes, where amateur orchid growers often attain the same results as experts employed at specialized horticultural firms.

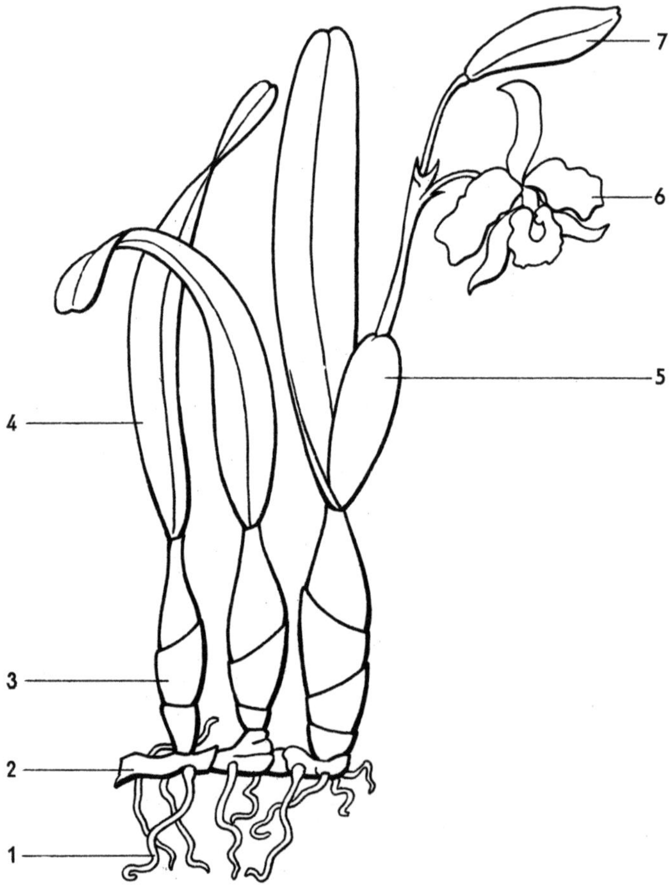

1. *Cattleya* — plant

1. Roots
2. Rhizome
3. Stem
4. Leaves
5. Receptacle
6. Flower
7. Bud

Orchidaceae

Orchidaceae is one of the largest plant families comprising about 600 genera and 18,000 species. We come across them, although rarely, right on the snowline where they grow in the form of ground plants. They grow as ground plants in the temperate zone too, but in this case they attain larger dimensions. Towards the Equator new varieties appear which grow epiphytically on trees.

Regarding form, orchids are very varied and are divided into three groups:

1. Orchids which have no organs for nutrient absorption either above or below ground (for example, the genus *Paphiopedilum* and genus *Phalaenopsis*). They are characterized by a very short period of rest after the vegetation period and they hardly stop growing. In cooler periods they require less moisture.

2. Orchids with organs—stems—above ground (for example, the genera *Cattleya*, *Dendrobium*, *Odontoglossum*). Their period of rest after vegetation occurs in the dry period, their source of water at such times being dew and moist air. Consequently their watering must not be neglected but, at the same time, it must not be carried out too often as the stems may shrivel.

3. Orchids with organs above ground and which lose their leaves or even roots in their period of rest after vegetation. An example of this group is *Calanthe*. In the dry period these varieties should be kept in absolutely dry and cool conditions.

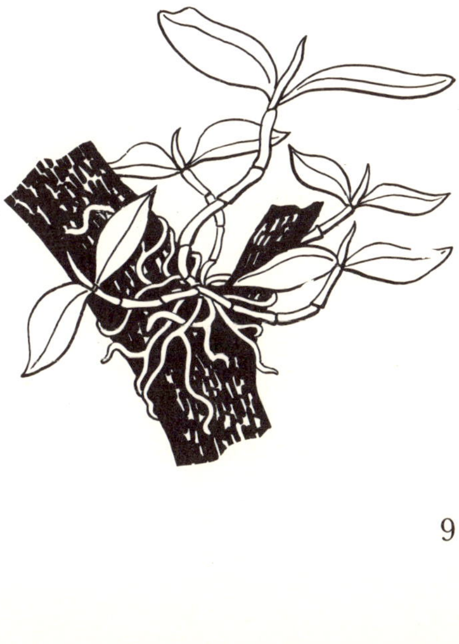

2. Epiphytic orchid growing on a branch

Orchids are further divided into categories according to their habitat, namely epiphytic, terrestrial or saprophytic. Epiphytic orchids live on the surface of other plants, mainly trees. They draw no nourishment from the trees, however, but absorb nutrients and moisture from the air through numerous pendent aerial roots. Terrestrial orchids are durable plants and have swollen underground stems or root tubers. Saprophytic orchids have no chlorophyll, are unable to synthesize organic compounds and they therefore depend upon absorbing organic compounds released during the decay of nearby vegetation.

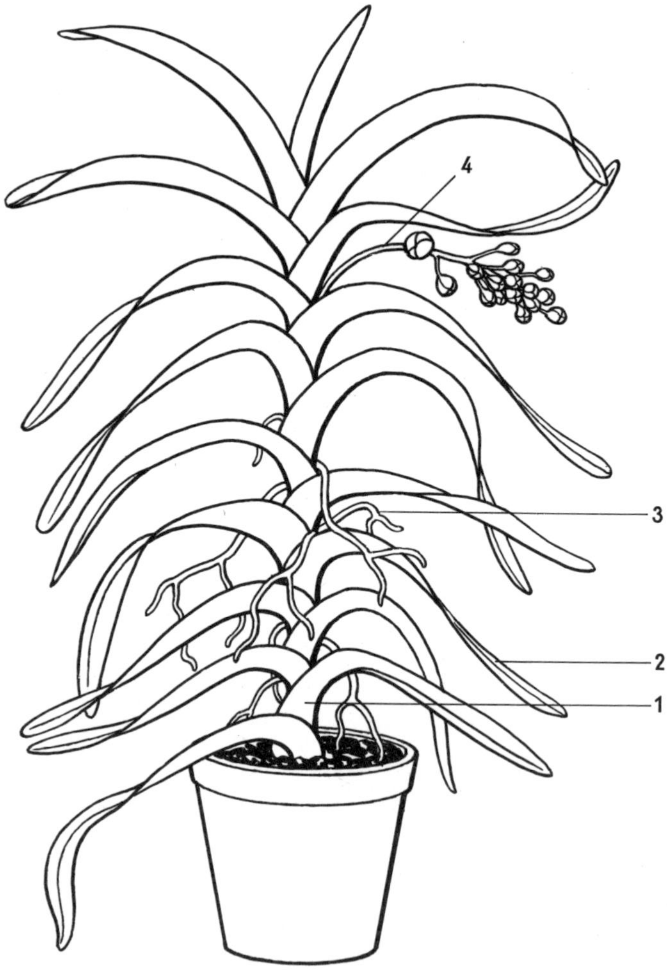

3. *Vanda* — plant

1. Stem
2. Leaves
3. Aerial roots
4. Flower stalk

The Blossoms and Fruits of Orchids

Orchid blossoms usually grow in grape-like clustered inflorescences situated symmetrically on both sides of the stalk. They have six petals of unequal size which are grouped in two whorls. The outer whorl are called sepals and are usually narrower and smaller than the inner whorl which are called petals. The largest of the petals forms a conspicuous labellum, which hangs downwards under its own weight, and often twists around the flower stalk. The labellum is usually divided into three parts. Sometimes the neighbouring flower petals attach themselves to it, thus forming a tree-platform. In other cases the labellum forms a spur of various lengths.

The fruit of an orchid is a capsule which usually bursts along six fissures. It contains a large number of tiny, powdery seeds which are covered with hygroscopic hairs and which are carried for large distances by the wind.

In the germination period the seeds increase in size to form protocorms on which tiny roots and buds later grow. It is interesting that the seeds germinate successfully and form protocorms which develop into perfect plants, only if there is a fungus present. In the case of artificial cultivation this fungus can be replaced by nutritive substances.

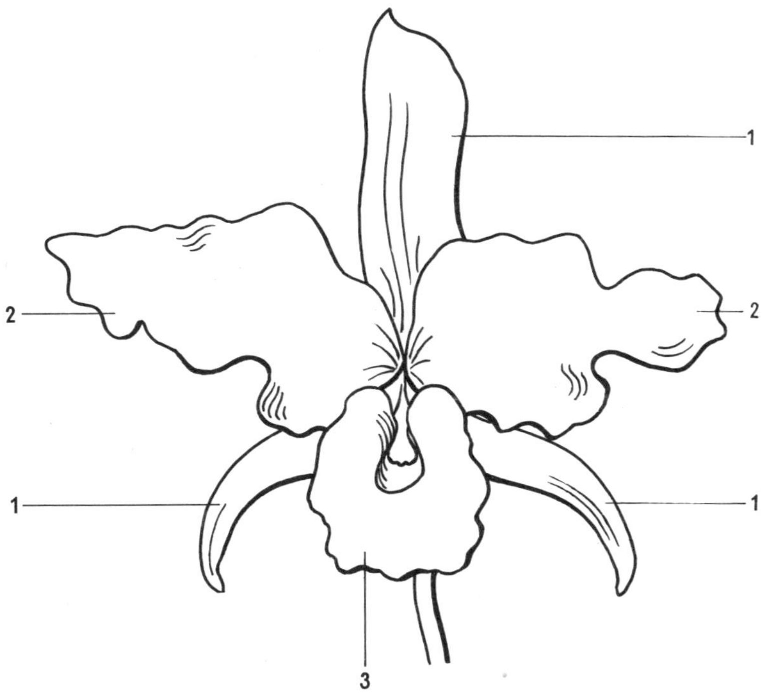

4. *Cattleya* — flower

1. Sepals
2. Petals
3. Labellum

Conditions for Growth

If orchids are cultivated in a greenhouse or in the home, care must be taken to ensure that conditions identical to those of their natural environment are provided. It is essential to maintain a higher temperature during the day and a lower temperature at night. The latter should always be from 3—5°C (5—9°F) lower than the day temperature. A higher day temperature is necessary during the synthesis of organic compounds and a lower night one for their breakdown. If this principle is not adhered to the orchids weaken and die. In general temperatures which are too extreme are harmful because the air either becomes disproportionally dry or its humidity increases rapidly. Consequently, the temperature must be adapted to the needs of the type of orchid cultivated. The best procedure is to consider the conditions that can be created for plant cultivation and then to choose a variety accordingly.

Orchids from tropical mountains 5,000—8,000 feet (1,500—3,000 metres) above sea level should be cultivated in a cold greenhouse. Varieties from lower regions and milder tropical zones are grown in a temperate greenhouse, while orchids coming directly from the tropics are cultivated in a hot greenhouse.

When growing more luxuriant cultures with a large number of varieties and different temperature requirements, it is advisable to have three sections in the greenhouse with different temperature conditions:

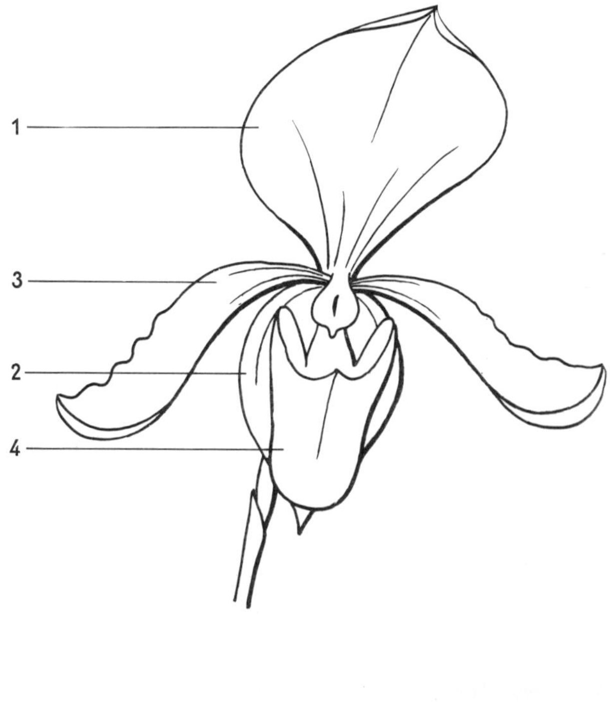

5. *Paphiopedilum* — flower

1. Upper sepals
2. Lower sepals
3. Petals
4. Labellum

a) a hot section: for *Cattleya* and *Laelia* varieties, several varieties of *Paphiopedilum*, *Phalaenopsis* and *Dendrobium* (throughout their vegetation period);

b) a temperate section: for the varieties *Paphiopedilum*, *Zygopetalum*, *Cymbidium*, *Coelogyne*, *Lycaste* and *Vanda* (throughout their vegetation period);

c) a cold section: for the varieties *Odontoglossum* and *Epidendrum* (throughout their vegetation period).

More detailed information about the temperatures required by the individual varieties is given in the plates section.

Table of monthly temperatures for the greenhouse sections in °C (°F)

	Hot Section		Temperate Section		Cold Section	
	Day	Night	Day	Night	Day	Night
January	16—18 (61—64)	14 (57)	12—14 (54—57)	10 (50)	8—10 (46—50)	6 (43)
February	16—18 (61—64)	14 (57)	12—14 (54—57)	10 (50)	8—10 (46—50)	4 (39)
March	16—18 (61—64)	14 (57)	12—14 (54—57)	10 (50)	10—12 (50—54)	8 (46)
April	18—20 (64—68)	16 (61)	14—16 (57—61)	12 (54)	12—14 (54—57)	10 (50)
May	20—22 (68—72)	18 (64)	16—18 (61—64)	14 (57)	14—16 (57—61)	12 (54)
June	22—24 (72—75)	20 (68)	20—22 (68—72)	16 (61)	16—18 (61—64)	14 (57)
July	22—24 (72—75)	20 (68)	20—22 (68—72)	16 (61)	16—18 (61—64)	14 (57)
August	22—24 (72—75)	20 (68)	20—22 (68—72)	16 (61)	16—18 (61—64)	14 (57)
September	20—22 (68—72)	18 (64)	18—20 (64—68)	14 (57)	14—16 (57—61)	12 (54)
October	18—20 (64—68)	16 (61)	18—20 (64—68)	14 (57)	12—14 (54—57)	10 (50)
November	16—18 (61—64)	14 (57)	16—18 (61—68)	12 (54)	10—12 (50—54)	8 (46)
December	16—18 (61—64)	14 (57)	14—16 (57—61)	12 (54)	8—10 (46—50)	6 (43)

Ventilation is an important factor in the cultivation of orchids. Perfect ventilation in the winter period is as important as fertilization for other plants — it has been said that orchids are the children of light and air. If it is too hot in the greenhouse or home a small amount of fresh air can be obtained by temperature regulation. However, it is necessary to bear in mind that a stream of fresh air is beneficial to plants only if it does not result in a sharp temperature change. Similarly, a draught is also harmful.

The most suitable means of ventilation is a small opening in the wall of the greenhouse. Air enters the greenhouse at ground level and circulates inside. It is fresh, warm, and damp. With the use of such a system air can be let into the greenhouse in any season of the year. The important point is to prevent it from blowing directly on to the plants and to ensure that it is first mixed and warmed up during the circulating process.

In many cases successful orchid cultivation depends on the type of floor used. In a greenhouse the soil under the tables should be loosened and the pathway can be sprinkled with sand. It is also advisable to scatter natural manure on the ground or to pour a manure solution over it as the resulting fumes foster growth of the plants. Open soil, dug once or twice a year, is the most suitable for orchid cultivation.

Watering is another very important factor. Well water is not suitable particularly in regions with a limestone base, rain water is far better. Water used for mist-spraying and watering should be at the same temperature as the atmosphere in the greenhouse. Cold water should never be used.

The degree of moisture in the air and the soil mixture should be adapted to the stage of development of the respective plants. In the non-vegetation period it should be lowered, while in the period of growth, and particularly when the temperature is higher, it should be raised proportionally. Orchids absorb moisture not only through their roots, but also through the surface of their leaves. The water requirements of the individual varieties as regards air humidity vary. Those which have strongly developed stems or which shed their leaves are used to a dry period in their natural habitat, while others of the evergreen type need a constant level of humidity in the non-vegetation period.

If a plant begins to grow and, in particular, if new roots appear, more frequent watering and mist-spraying are necessary. On completion of growth a plant needs less water and consequently watering need not be carried out so frequently. In some cases it can even be stopped entirely for a short time before the blossoming period. These finer points of orchid cultivation will be discussed separately for each variety.

An orchid grower soon learns to recognize the humidity of the air in his greenhouse. If the air is dry it must be moistened. This involves pouring water over the tables between the flowerpots and also over the walls and passages. Although the plants are watered and sprayed with rain water, ordinary mains water may be used for pouring over the walls and paths. The air-moistening process should be repeated several times daily in every greenhouse.

Plant-spraying is started in spring when the sunlight becomes stronger. Initially it should be done only at noon, and in May twice a day. For the rest of the summer spraying should be carried out three times a day, namely in the morning, at noon, and in the evening. When the weather is rainy or cool spraying can be done less frequently and only in the morning. A good guide for correct watering is *Sphagnum* moss or the leaves of wall-fern. If the *Sphagnum* on the top of flowerpots or the wall-fern in baskets is bright green it means that the particular plant has sufficient moisture, but when it is light green it indicates that watering is necessary.

Orchid growers who wish to enhance their collection with more sensitive varieties should introduce 'terrarium cultures' in their homes, namely cultivation in glass cases or vessels situated as near as possible to a window. The flowerpots should be placed on a fairly thick layer of *Sphagnum*. Ground types, on the other hand, thrive better if their flowerpots are sunk in moss. The terrarium should be covered with a sheet of glass which makes easy and regular ventilation possible. An electric light bulb or small heating body should be placed below the metal base of the terrarium for heating purposes. Even the most sensitive varieties of orchid grow and blossom well in such an environment. Cultivated plants grown in this way should be mist-sprayed in the vegetation period. This should be done several times a day, but particularly in the morning, so that the plants are dry during the night. If orchids are grown in large glass cases, glass window boxes, or freely in the home, the moisture of the air round the plants should also be increased by spraying. Apart from this the same principles apply for watering, temperature and ventilation as in the case of greenhouse cultivation.

Different varieties of orchid require different intensities of light. Those varieties whose hosts are solitary growing trees or which grow on rocks require more light than those which grow on the ground and in the tops of trees. Epiphytic varieties push their way through narrow bends in the branches and through the leaves of their hosts, thus gaining sufficient light while simultaneously protected against the hot rays of the sun. Other varieties, characterized by short stalks and small, tough leaves, thrive in unshaded light. This is possible in natural conditions as the access of fresh air prevents overheating. If orchids are cultivated under glass, however, a slight amount of shade must be provided for them. In summer, during the middle of the day, it is necessary to shade all varieties of orchids. In general it can be said that those varieties which have stems require light, and those with soft leaves prefer shade.

The orchid requiring the largest amount of light is *Dendrobium*, followed by *Cattleya*, *Laelia*, *Cymbidium*, *Oncidium* and *Vanda* varieties. *Paphiopedilum*, *Phalaenopsis*, *Odontoglossum*, *Miltonia* and *Stanhopea* require less light. Great attention should be paid to the shading of plants in spring, when this procedure is started, but it should be stopped in autumn. During the winter months, in the moist and hot air, together with an inadequate amount of light, orchid plants become more sensitive, and the warm spring sunlight would be harmful. Shading should always stop about mid-October unless the weather remains sunny for a longer period. In such a case it should continue, especially in the case of plants placed near glass, as they would otherwise be liable to considerable damage.

However, over-shading is also incorrect, whether by a layer of lime on the glass or some other kind of shade. It is best to allow light to penetrate into the greenhouse towards the evening and to shade it again in the morning. On overcast or rainy days shading is not necessary. Shades made of narrow wooden laths or slats and placed about 12 inches (30 centimetres) from the glass have proved highly practical. Dispersed light falls on the plants and at the same time air flows across the glass, lowering the temperature inside the greenhouse. Both these results are beneficial to the plants.

When orchids are grown in glass window-boxes those varieties requiring sunlight should be placed in a sunny position and those requiring less light should be located in a more shaded spot. When cultivating orchids in the home the danger of over exposure does not arise, as it does in a greenhouse, because excessive light is rarely present in such an environment. The plants should be shaded only if it is found that their leaves are warm. It is merely necessary to lower the blind to provide the necessary shade but it must be raised as soon as the strong sunlight disappears.

In autumn it is necessary to provide the plants with shade only at mid-day but apart from this they should have as much light as possible in order to grow.

In the autumn and winter months artificial lighting is also beneficial. A normal electric bulb or neon tube may be used and should be switched on as soon as the sun sets and left for a maximum of two hours. A longer period of illumination would be disadvantageous.

Care of Orchids Imported from the Tropics

If orchid plants are received directly from the Tropics particular measures must be adopted to ensure their healthy growth. The orchids should be unpacked outside the greenhouse in order to prevent destructive insects from entering with the plants, and attacking species already present. Every plant must be inspected separately and all dead leaves and stems removed. The plants should then be submerged for a short time in an insecticide solution and then placed on *Sphagnum* in boxes and housed in a mildly warm greenhouse. When the first new roots appear, the plants should be transferred to flowerpots and cared for in the normal manner.

Soil

Cultivated orchids are divided into two groups according to their growth form. Included in the first group are those varieties which, in their natural habitat, grow in the ground. These are called terrestrial varieties. The second group comprises the species that grow on trees and produce aerial roots through which they absorb moisture. These are known as epiphytes.

When growing orchids in a greenhouse the soil in which they are planted must be adapted to the conditions prevailing in their natural environment. In order that the maximum amount of air may reach the roots of epiphytes a light but rough mixture must be chosen. Many mixtures have been experimented with, but the best results are obtained by the use of the roots of ferns of *Osmunda regalis* and *Polypodium vulgare* species, the moss *Sphagnum squarrosum* and undecayed beech leaves. The mixture usually used for epiphytes consists of one third *Polypodium* or *Osmunda*, one third beech leaves and one third *Sphagnum* with the addition of a few pieces of charcoal. The moisture content is indicated by the *Sphagnum*, and accordingly a larger amount of *Polypodium* or *Osmunda* and less *Sphagnum* is used, or vice versa. In the case of the genera *Dendrobium*, *Phalaenopsis* and *Vanda* the mixture should contain a larger amount of *Osmunda* or *Polypodium*, the genera *Cattleya*, *Bulbophyllum*, *Epidendrum*, *Oncidium* and *Odontoglossum* requiring a larger amout of *Sphagnum*.

In recent years use has been made in Europe of dead pine bark as a supplement to the mixture and good results have been obtained in all cases. This bark-containing mixture is prepared as follows: one part *Polypodium* or *Osmunda*, one part *Sphagnum*, one part beech leaves and one part pine bark.

In the case of terrestrial orchids one part compost or clods of loam can be added. However, care should be taken to ensure that the permeability of the soil is not affected by the addition of pure soils. If too much soil is added to the orchid mixture it will cease to be open and porous and will prevent water from draining freely and air from moving through the compost and about the roots. It is only very rarely that orchids can be grown in a mixture composed entirely of soil, materials of a more fibrous nature being more commonly used instead.

Flowerpots and Baskets

Vessels used for the cultivation of orchids may be of various shapes. For small plants earthen flowerpots may be used, but for larger types bowls are more suitable. By far the best are flowerpots and bowls with holes in their walls, since orchids require a constant supply of air to their soil. The flowerpots must always be clean and if new ones are obtained, they must be soaked in water for a considerable period before use.

Large, strong plants, particularly epiphytes, should be planted in lath baskets of different sizes. Quite small baskets of this kind can be made and used instead of flowerpots. Orchids which form longer stems can be planted in suitably adapted pieces of bark or cork. The soil can be held round their roots using rust-proof wire. Plants cultivated in bark require additional watering and fertilization.

Transplanting Orchids

For orchids, transplanting is quite a critical process and as the vegetation cycle of different genera varies it is not possible to state a particular time at which it should be carried out. Consequently only general hints can be given on this matter. The reader will find more detailed advice in the description of the individual cultures.

As a rule orchids are transplanted after their blossoms have faded, namely at the beginning of their new vegetation period, which in the case of some varieties is in spring and in others summer or autumn. New growth is manifested by an increase in the size of the buds and the appearance of new roots. Very often, however, the cultures of a single variety start growing at different times. Only those plants which have started to grow should be transplanted, and this means that the process is a gradual one. Provided the soil in the flowerpots is good and shows no sign of decay, transplantation need not be carried out every year. As a rule it is usually done when the rootstock grows above the rim of the flowerpot.

Flowerpots, bowls and baskets intended for the transplantation of orchids, as well as the broken pieces of glass or china serving for drainage purposes, should be well cleaned. Dirty vessels must never be used. The roots of some varieties cling to the walls of their flowerpots or, if planted in baskets, to the wooden laths. In the case of a particularly sensitive variety such as *Phalaenopsis* it is advisable to cut out the roots carefully together with the wood and replant them. Before doing so, however, all old useless tubers and dead roots must be removed.

The rootstock of orchid plants need not be planted deep in the soil and care should be taken that the new growing shoot is in the centre of the flowerpot or basket (see illustration 6). If the rootstock is too long, it can be wound round the flowerpot in such a way that the new shoot is orientated towards the middle. The soil mixture should be well mixed and placed in the flowerpots gradually, in small amounts, to prevent the formation of large air spaces. In view of the fact that transplantation is sometimes carried out after two or three years and that soil is subject to decay, it is essential to plant the orchids in such a way that, when taken by the leaves and shaken, the plants do not move in the soil.

When transplanted, orchids should be sprayed but not watered direct. Renewal of the root growth indicates that the plants have started to vegetate. Only then should the moisture content of the air be gradually increased up to the normal level. In the case of plants cultivated in the home, supplementary lighting by means of an electric light bulb is beneficial after transplantation.

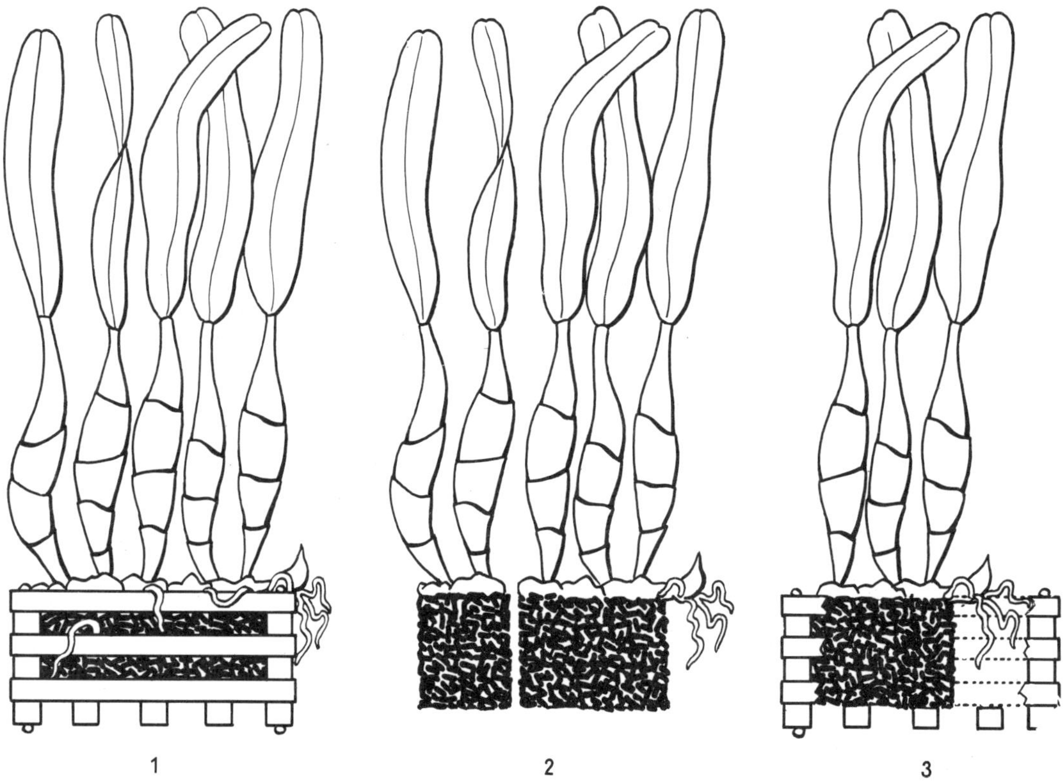

6. Transplantation of Orchid

1. Plant before transplantation
2. Plant divided for transplantation
3. The correctly transplanted plant

Feeding Orchids

When growing in their natural environment orchids obtain nourishment from water vapour in the air as well from the dead bark of the trees to which their roots are attached. Another occasional source of nourishment is bird droppings. This could have given rise to the opinion that orchids do not require extra fertilization when grown in cultures. A number of tests has shown, however, that fertilization is of great importance for their growth and inflorescences, especially when the latter are required as rich as possible. A suitable organic fertilizer consists of a weak solution of manure which should be used alternately with a weak solution of inorganic fertilizers. The latter has an advantage over organic fertilizers in that it can be prepared in more convenient concentrations. As a rule, small amounts of inorganic fertilizers are used in the same way as when sowing seeds in the ground. A suitable solution of inorganic nutrients can be prepared by dissolving the following in 10 litres of rain water:

Chemical	Formula	Weight (gm)
calcium nitrate	$Ca(NO_3)_2$	1·00
magnesium sulphate crystals	$MgSO_4$	0·25
primary potassium phosphate	KN_2PO_4	0·25
ammonium sulphate	$(NH_4)_2SO_4$	0·50
ferrous sulphate	$FeSO_4$	0·25
manganese sulphate	$MnSO_4$	0·0075

This basic list gives the proportions of the individual components of the solution and naturally should a larger volume be required, the individual amounts should be proportionately increased. Only healthy plants should be fertilized, and only during the vegetation period. The same solution can also be used for leaf-spraying, since orchid plants absorb, through their leaves, a relatively large amount of substances dissolved in water. Nutrient solutions can likewise be used to spray plants with damaged roots and on young seedlings to promote their growth. Tests have also proved the beneficial effect of the fumes arising from organic fertilizers, and it is therefore advantageous to place buckets of strong manure solution under the tables on which the flowerpots are placed.

Harmful Insects and Diseases

Orchids bring harmful insects and diseases from their natural habitats and consequently all imported plants are subjected to strict inspections. New varieties bred at specialized establishments are more resistant to disease. In addition, modern protective measures are more efficient than those formerly used with the result that harmful insects and diseases occur less frequently.

Very widespread insects with a harmful effect include certain sucking species such as the grubs of the genera *Diaspis*, *Espidiotus* and *Lepidosaphes* which settle on the leaves of orchid plants and the dry lodicules of their roots. The simplest means of protection consists of washing and brushing the effected places, followed by spraying with an organo-phosphorous insecticide such as phosdrine (70 gm in 100 litres of water).

The multiplication of the genus *Helothrips* is encouraged by dry air, these insects sucking both leaves and blossoms with the result that brown spots appear on the plants. Such damage can be prevented by means of a malathion, parathion or phosdrine spray (90 gm in 100 litres of water).

Considerable damage is caused to orchid cultures by certain kinds of snail which feed on young buds, leaves, grown buds and blossoms. Most susceptible to such damage are plants placed on tables. For this reason poisoned bait should be placed in the vicinity of the flowerpots to attract snails away from the plants. To protect the buds and blossoms dry cotton wool can be wound round the stalks.

When placed in an environment with inadequate air circulation or an over-moist and hot atmosphere, orchids suffer from a number of fungus diseases causing for example the appearance of black spots on their leaves. Leaves affected in this way can be improved by spraying with a fungicide such as captan or zinep in the dosage indicated by the manufacturer. Certain varieties, such as *Phalaenopsis*, are susceptible to bacterial diseases caused by the genus *Ervinia*, and the genus *Cattleya* is prone to attack from the parasitic genus *Phytomonas-Cattleyae*. In such instances the leaves of the damaged plants slowly turn brown and wither.

Orchids are also attacked by virus diseases which cause the gradual yellowing of the leaves and the withering of the plants. Orchids thus affected should be isolated or even burned.

Propagation of Orchids

Vegetative Propagation

Orchids are usually propagated by division, usually through the rootstock. Large plants should be divided in the places where the rootstock branches out. The part intended for separation should have at least three healthy roots of which two should always be covered with leaves. Rather than carrying out the dividing process immediately, preliminary preparations should be made one year beforehand. Before the beginning of the vegetation period in spring or in winter, the rootstock should be cut where a new shoot is required. At first it should be cut only half-way through, and the cut completed when a new shoot grows from the dormant bud. The new shoot forms its own roots. In the case of large, strong plants several cuts can be made which result in the growth of a large number of new shoots, making possible their division into many plants. This method of propagation is applicable particularly in the case of the genera *Cattleya*, *Laelia*, *Cymbidium*, *Zygopetalum*, *Coelogyne*, *Epidendrum*, and others.

As regards the genera *Cymbidium* and *Odontoglossum* and, in rarer cases, *Zygopetalum*, old leafless tubers should be cut and set in individual flowerpots, using a soil mixture of *Sphagnum* and sand. After one year new, strong shoots grow from the divided tubers which should then be transplanted in the appropriate mixture.

Strong plants of the genus *Paphiopedilum* are propagated by division as soon as their flowerpots are full of grown roots. Some varieties grow from the centre in a circular manner. The middle part of the plant dies and in the course of transplantation it disintegrates into several parts. Hybrid *Cypripediums* grow more slowly and branch out less richly with the result that their propagation is more difficult. In their case too, rapid multiplication is encouraged by gently pulling the rootstock away from the old shoots. Following this new shoots appear on the old parts of the plant. When transplanting care should be taken not to divide very young and small shoots. In such cases it takes years before these young shoots grow into large plants capable of producing blossoms. Each separated part of a plant must have at least two or three shoots, and by applying this method the original number of plants can be doubled within five years.

A particularly interesting method of vegetative propagation is used for certain varieties of *Dendrobium*, especially *Dendrobium nobile* and its hybrids. If the non-vegetation period is disregarded it often happens that *Dendrobium* grows little plants with roots on the leaf stalks instead of blossoms. As a rule these little plants are left to grow for one year, and are then separated and set in small flowerpots in the course of the following year. When propagated in this way *Dendrobium* blossoms in the third year.

Generative Propagation

Before orchid growers were acquainted with scientific methods of propagation they planted seeds in the soil surrounding the parent plant. Many plants were cultivated in this way, but the majority of the seeds failed to germinate. The main disadvantage lay in the fact that the seeds were not set in a sterile environment and sown seeds growing above the agar or moss were washed away when watered. In some places this method is still used, for example for the genus *Paphiopedilum*, but even here, scientific measures are now finding application.

a) *Symbiotic Sowing of Seeds*

Before the First World War growers became interested in the cultivation of orchids from seeds, and it was at that time that French botanist Professor N. Bernard succeeded in growing the first orchid fungus in nutrient soil. He planted orchid seeds in a fungus culture and witnessed their successful germination, this phenomen demonstrating the symbiosis of a fungus and an orchid plant. Professor Hans Burgeff of Würzburg in Germany continued the work of Professor N. Bernard and isolated fungi from other types of orchid. He discovered new nutrient solutions and soils for the individual types of fungus, and on the basis of oft-repeated experiments worked out a planting process which he named the symbiotic process.

Professor Burgeff isolated the fungus living inside the root cells and grafted it onto the surface of the nutrient soil, thus acquiring a fungus culture on whose surface he planted orchid seeds. In order to prevent contamination of the seeds, he carried out the whole procedure under perfectly sterile conditions.

If small, well grown plants are available which were cultivated symbiotically, it is sufficient to plant them in nutrient soil instead of grafting the fungus. A fungus grows by itself in nutrient soil and encourages the germination and good growth of the seeds. After the elapse of one year or more the small plants should be pressed into flat earthen bowls.

b) *Asymbiotic Planting of Seeds*

Dr. Lewis Knudson of Cornel University in the U.S.A. studied the work of

Professor N. Bernard and Professor H. Burgeff and, in 1921, arrived at the conclusion that a symbiotic fungus produces sugars for the initial development of an orchid embryo. He therefore prepared some soils containing sugar and other nutrients and achieved a high germination rate, proving that it is possible to cultivate orchids from seeds without a symbiotic fungus. At the same time he also described a number of suitable nutrient soils. Dr. Knudson's asymbiotic method has proved of great value not only in specialized orchid-growing establishments, but also among amateur growers.

1. *Preparation of Glassware*

The most suitable containers for sowing orchid seeds are Erlenmayer flasks. These should be washed well with soap, rinsed in distilled water and closed with a stopper of cellulose wadding wrapped in a thin layer of gauze. Such stoppers should be wrapped in paper and sterilized in hot air at a temperature of 140°C (284°F) for ninety minutes.

2. *Preparation of Nutrient Soil*

Finely cut or powdered agar (17·5 gm) should be placed in a 1 litre Erlenmayer flask. To this should be added 900 ml of distilled water. The contents of the flask must then be shaken and left to stand for about two hours in a cool place. After this period the water should be poured off and fresh water added, and the whole process of washing the agar repeated two or three times. Following this the agar should be boiled in the same amount of water and left to stand overnight. The next day the following nutrients should be dissolved in 100 ml of distilled water:

Chemical	Formula	Weight (gm)
Calcium nitrate	$Ca(NO_3)_2$	1·00
Primary potassium phosphate	KN_2PO_4	0·25
Magnesium sulphate crystals	$MgSO_4$	0·25
Ammonium sulphate	$(NH_4)_2SO_4$	0·50
Ferrous sulphate	$FeSO_4$	0·05

This solution should be poured into the flasks with the dissolved agar and 20 gm of beet sugar added. This nutrient solution must be strained through gauze and poured into sterilized flasks. These are then provided with stoppers, bound in cellophane and sterilized in steam for twenty minutes. One litre of nutrient soil is sufficient for twenty flasks.

3. *Planting the Seeds*

Seeds from ripe but unburst seed capsules are suitable for planting. The capsule should be washed in disinfectant and cut carefully with a sterilized scalpel. If the capsule has opened already the seeds must be disinfected using a one percent chlorine solution. The seeds are planted in flasks containing nutrient soil using a platinum needle. The flasks must be provided with stoppers and bound in cellophane. The cultivation flasks containing the seeds, and later on the seedlings, must be kept in a warm and moist environment, and consequently mould can easily grow on the wrapping. The cellophane should therefore be soaked in the one percent chlorine solution before being wound round the stoppers and bound with cord similarly prepared.

4. *Placing the Flasks in the Greenhouse*

The flasks containing pure orchid cultures should be placed in a mildly moist and mildly shaded greenhouse in which a temperature of 22—25°C (72—77°F) prevails. In sunny weather it is advisable to ventilate the greenhouse well at mid-day. Within one month after planting the seeds small, round seedlings usually appear which must remain in the flasks for another year. After this period they can be placed in normal soil.

For the seedlings, sterilized earthen bowls must be prepared and should be filled to one half of their weight with porcelain chips, and the remaining space with a mixture of two parts peat soil, one part ground charcoal, two parts *Sphagnum* and one part sand. Level the surface of the soil mixture and prick out relatively closely spaced holes in which to plant the seedlings. The bowls containing the seedlings should then be placed in a hot, shaded greenhouse and watering carried out with rain water as required. Six to eight months from their planting in the bowls, the seedlings should have normal white roots. Orchid plants which are transferred from flasks to normal soil require a great amount of attention and it is essential to protect them from insect attacks by the use of insecticides.

When the seedlings become strong they should be transplanted in flowerpots 2 inches (5 centimetres) in diameter, in a small quantity of the soil in which they originally grew. Timely transplanting is important in order to prevent the seedlings from forming over-long roots in the bowls. Should this point be neglected the long roots would break during the transplanting process. It is also advisable to place the flowerpots containing the transplanted seedlings in *Sphagnum*, to prevent them from drying up, and to provide artificial light in the early morning and evening. Today all kinds of orchids can be cultivated by using pure cultures.

What has been said so far represents a summary of the basic principles governing the cultivation of orchids. Some readers may think that the process is very complicated, but the successes achieved by amateurs witness the fact that orchids can be cultivated well not only in greenhouses, but also in the home. If the reader looks at the plates of this book and examines the specimens carefully he will soon become enchanted by them and gladly sacrifice a little effort in order to enjoy their exquisiteness in his own home.

PLATES

Ada

These are epiphytic orchids with densely growing, elongated stalks 4 inches (10 centimetres) high. One or two leaves 6—8 inches (15—20 centimetres) long grow from the stalks, and the cluster of blossoms, usually pendent, is of the same length.

Ada orchids are suitable for a cold greenhouse. They should be transplanted only in spring when they form new roots in the soil mixture for epiphytic orchids. Small flowerpots with good drainage are recommended. After they have been transplanted the orchids should not be watered for three weeks by which time new roots should have appeared. Watering and spraying should be carried out with regard to the weather. During the summer months the plants must be shaded well as they do not grow well in a high temperature. As soon as the plants have well developed shoots their watering should be restricted but when the flower stalk appears watering can be restarted. Apart from this the genus *Ada* is cultivated following the principles applicable to the genus *Odontoglossum* (see page 96).

A. aurantiaca (LDL.) This variety comes from New Granada. It has a long, slender leaf stem which grows to a height of about 4 inches (10 centimetres) and has two leaves 6—8 inches (15—20 centimetres) long. The flower stalk is 8 inches (20 centimetres) high with a cluster of as many as twelve blossoms.

A. lehmannii (ROLFE.) This orchid came originally from Colombia and grows more richly than the preceding type. The leaves are elongated, leathery, dark green and marble patterned in grey. The flower stalk is 10 inches (25 centimetres) long and straight, and usually bears eight to ten blossoms. The latter are orange-red in colour with a white labellum and appear in August to September.

Ada aurantiaca

Aerangis

The members of the genus *Aerangis* are epiphytic orchids which have no leaf stalks. Some varieties have short stems. Their blossoms are mostly white or slightly yellowish and grow in rich clusters. They come from tropical America and particularly from Madagascar.

These orchids are not suitable for cutting but are very suitable for cultivation by amateurs as their growth is rich and compact. Some varieties blossom in the winter period and others in summer. After the flowering period the plants cease to vegetate and consequently the surrounding temperature should be lowered and watering carried out less frequently. In winter the plants require a temperature of 18—20°C (64—68°F), but in summer it should be higher.

These orchids look very attractive when attached to cork or branches and roots but can also be grown in small baskets or flowerpots. *Aerangis* species should not be transplanted often. If attached to branches it is necessary only to provide the orchids with fresh soil, but otherwise they should be transplanted in the mixture suitable for epiphytic orchids, before the renewal of their growth. Due to their abundant growth they are suitable for small window greenhouses or for glass show-cases.

A. articulatum (SCHLTR.) This orchid has a short stem and oval shaped leaves which are 3—5 inches (7·5—12 centimetres) long and 1—1½ inches (2·5—4 centimetres) wide. The blossoming period occurs from July to August and the snow-white blossoms up to 14 inches (35 centimetres) long and 1 inch (2·5 centimetres) wide, grow in dense clusters.

A. citratum (SCHLTR.) This orchid has long, oval leaves which are 1—1½ inches (2·5—4 centimetres) wide and as much as 5 inches (12 centimetres) long. The flowers are yellow-white, 1 inch (2·5 centimetres) across and they appear in February and up to April.

A. modestum (SCHLTR.) This variety greatly resembles *A. articulatum*. The leaves are 4—6 inches (10—15 centimetres) long and the snow-white blossoms grow in dense, hanging clusters, as much as 1 inch (2·5 centimetres) wide. This orchid flowers from February to April.

Aerangis citratum

Aerides

This genus comprises epiphytic orchids without shoots and with a stem bearing leathery leaves with strong, aerial roots growing from their stalks. The flower stalk grows from the axils of the leaves and bears hanging clusters of beautiful blossoms. Fifty different varieties originate from tropical Asia.

Larger varieties should be grown in a hot greenhouse in flowerpots, a cold environment rarely being suitable. Large orchid plants should always be transplanted after three to four years and spring is the best time since it is then that the roots renew their growth. Soil for epiphytic orchids should be used. In summer, when the plants are well rooted, a higher temperature should be maintained in the greenhouse together with a higher degree of humidity. The plants should also be lightly shaded. During the winter months the ambient temperature can be lowered to 16—18°C (61—64°F) and watering carried out only to an extent to prevent the leaves from shrivelling.

A. odoratum (LOUR.) This variety comes from India and China. It has thong-like leaves as much as 8 inches (20 centimetres) long which grow densely in two rows on their stalk. The blossoms are 1 inch (2·5 centimetres) across and form luxuriant, strongly perfumed clusters. The petals and sepals are oval, white in colour, with a pinkish-red spot at their tips. The funnel-shaped labellum has a purple stripe in its centre. The flowers blossom in June and July.

A. vandarum (RCHB. F.) This plant comes from the Himalayas. The leaves are narrow and 8 inches (20 centimetres) long. The flower stalks are short and bear two to four white blossoms which are 1½—2 inches (4—5 centimetres) across. The petals and sepals are widely elliptic in shape and have wavy edges, while the long, pointed labellum is trilobate. This orchid flowers from February to March.

Aerides vandarum

Angraecum

This is a genus of epiphytic orchids with a short, densely leafed stem. The blossoms are of various sizes, but most of them form clusters, although some varieties have single blossoms. About fifty varieties grow in Africa and Madagascar. Due to its special characteristics and extraordinary beauty, this genus is particularly suitable for inclusion in growers' collections.

Angraecum varieties should be grown in a hot, shaded environment the temperature of which should be 18—20°C (64—68°F) in winter and somewhat lower in summer. These plants thrive well in moist, fresh air and during their vegetation period they require thorough watering and frequent spraying. At the conclusion of the vegetation period they should be watered sparingly, but their root-mass must never be allowed to dry up completely. Some varieties flower in winter and spring and others in summer. The *Angraecum* orchid should always be transplanted before the beginning of the vegetation period, using the soil mixture suitable for epiphytic orchids. If the stem of the plant has no leaves at its base the leafy top can be cut and the roots carefully coiled and planted fairly deeply in a flowerpot or basket. The surface of the soil should then be covered with fresh *Sphagnum*. Most varieties grow to a large size and can therefore be cultivated in the home, if there is sufficient space.

A. eburneum (BORY.) These orchids have relatively thick stems and very thick, leathery leaves up to 2 feet (60 centimetres) long and 2 inches (5 centimetres) wide. Individual blossoms are 4 inches (10 centimetres) wide and grow in clusters. The petals and sepals are light green and the labellum white. The plant flowers in December and January and comes from Madagascar.

A. sesquipedale (THOU.) This variety has a thick 40 inches (1 metre) high stalk, densely covered with leaves. The clusters of flowers have only two to four blossoms but this orchid has the largest blossoms of the whole genus. They are 6—7 inches (15—18 centimetres) wide and ivory-white in colour. This orchid flowers from December to April and originally came from Madagascar.

Angraecum eburneum

Anguloa

This genus comprises epiphytic orchids which grow on moss-covered rocks. The leaf stem is short with two or three leaves. The upright flower stalk usually bears one blossom. About nine varieties come from Colombia and Peru. Hybrids obtained by crossing the genus *Anguloa* and the genus *Lycaste* are known as *Angulocastes*.

Orchids of the genus *Anguloa* are often cultivated in the home, and highly valued in the collections of amateur growers. They thrive best in a mild, shady environment as a high temperature is detrimental to their growth. The orchids should be planted in soil suitable for epiphytic orchids with an addition of humus, and subsequently placed in a temperature of 15—16°C (59—61°F). In March new shoots begin to grow, often from old rootstocks.

During the vegetation period occasional watering with a weak cow-manure solution proves beneficial to these orchids. The leaves of old roots die, and only the youngest remain. On completion of their growth these orchids require a drier atmosphere for the non-vegetation period, which begins in October and ends in December. Spring witnesses the growth of the blossoms and it is then that new roots and leaves appear.

A. clowesii (LDL.) The stalks of this orchid are 3—5½ inches (7·5—14 centimetres) high and have two to four leaves which are 20 inches (50 centimetres) long and elliptic with pointed ends. The middle flower stem is 12 inches (30 centimetres) long, the blossoms are lemon-yellow in colour and strongly perfumed. This variety comes from Colombia and flowers in April and May.

A. ruckeri (LDL.) In appearance this orchid resembles the previously described variety. It has short, but thicker stalks. The blossoms are olive green on their outer sides and yellow with densely situated reddish-brown spots on their inner sides. The labellum is brownish-red.

Anguloa clowesii

Anoectochilus

This genus comprises ground orchids with soft, creeping rootstocks and beautifully coloured leaves. The flower stalk is upright and about 6 inches (15 centimetres) high while the blossoms are small and white. The home of this genus is India. The genus *Anoectochilus* greatly resembles the genus *Haemaria*, hybrids obtained by cross-breeding are called *Anoectomaria*.

Together with the genera *Dossinia*, *Macodes* and *Haemaria*, the genus *Anoectochilus* forms a group of tropical ground orchids. They are not suitable for cultivation if their blossoms are to be cut. Nevertheless, they are very popular with amateur orchid-growers and thrive best in window greenhouses or in glass show-cases. The individual flowerpots can also be placed under glass covers. These plants require a high temperature, about 20°C (68°F) in winter and higher in the vegetation period in summer, very moist air, and shade. Their soft pulpy rootstock should be planted in flat bowls with good drainage and several rootstocks can be set in one bowl. The most suitable soil is a mixture of *Sphagnum*, *Polypodium* or *Osmunda*, beech-leaf mould and pieces of charcoal. The bowls in which the plants are set should be placed in larger bowls containing *Sphagnum*. These orchids should not be sprayed as the necessary humidity is provided by moistening the moss.

A. regalis (BL.) This orchid grows in Ceylon in the humus of mountain forests and it reaches a height of 10 inches (25 centimetres). The flower stalk bears a large number of blossoms 1 inch (2·5 centimetres) long which are green with a white labellum. The outer side of the leaves is dark green with light gold veins, and the leaves themselves have a velvet-like texture. The plant flowers from April to June.

A. setaceus (BL.) This variety comes from Java and greatly resembles the previously described type. The petals and sepals are green with brownish-red tips and the labellum is white. The leaves have a velvet-like texture and are greenish-black with silver veins. The plant bossoms from April to June.

Anoectochilus regalis

Bifrenaria

The orchids of the genus *Bifrenaria* are epiphytic and have subovate stalks bearing one leathery leaf. The blossoms resemble those of *Lycaste* and grow in clusters. The home of the majority of the twenty-five varieties is Brazil, others growing in Venezuela and Guyana.

All varieties of the genus *Bifrenaria* are cultivated in a moderate or cold greenhouse and are planted in a soil mixture suitable for epiphytic orchids, with an addition of peat. They should be transplanted after the blossoming period, following which they should be hardly watered until they begin to grow new roots. During the peak vegetation period they may be watered several times with a weak fertilizer solution. The cultivation of these orchids is not very exacting as they grow easily, flower regularly, and are consequently very popular with amateur orchid growers.

B. atropurpurea (LDL.) This variety has subovate stems about 2—2½ inches (5—7 centimetres) high, bearing one leaf. The leaves can be up to 10 inches (25 centimetres) long and pointed. The cluster of blossoms is about 3 inches (8 centimetres) long with three to five flowers which are up to 2 inches (5 centimetres) wide. The petals and sepals are oval, red coloured with a yellow centre, while the labellum is oblong, wavy in front and pinkish-red in colour. This variety blossoms in June.

B. harrisoniae (RCHB. F.) This variety has subovate, angular stems up to 3 inches (8 centimetres) high with pointed leaves up to 12 inches (30 centimetres) long. The cluster of blossoms is short with two to three flowers which can be 2½ inches (7 centimetres) wide. The petals and sepals are oval and blunt, with their tips yellow, while the labellum is purplish-red with its inner part red with yellow hairs. The plant blossoms in March and April.

Bifrenaria harrisoniae

Brassavola

This genus of epiphytic orchids is very similar to the genus *Laelia*. The two genera can be distinguished only by their fruits, which in the case of the genus *Brassavola* are long and pointed. The varieties of this genus have thin stalks terminating in fleshy, rounded leaves. The blossoms are white with a greenish or yellow tint with narrow projecting petals and sepals, and a simple labellum. They usually grow singly or from short clusters. The genus *Brassavola* comprises about fifteen varieties whose original home was tropical America. As with *Cattleya*, they should be cultivated in a greenhouse of moderate temperature (see text on pages 52 and 54).

B. digbyana (LDL.) This variety has club-shaped, slightly flat stems which grow to a height of 6 inches (15 centimetres) and bear one leaf. This is about 8 inches (20 centimetres) long and somewhat fleshy. The blossoms are 4—4½ inches (10—12 centimetres) wide, sweet-smelling, and grow individually on short stalks. The sepals are strap-shaped and 2 inches (5 centimetres) long, and the petals are pinkish and wider. The labellum is creamy white, indented and frayed at its edges. This variety blossoms in May. It comes from Honduras and its cross-breeding with the genus *Cattleya* has given rise to numerous hybrids.

B. glauca (LDL.) This orchid has slender stems with leaves about 6 inches (15 centimetres) long. The blossoms, which grow individually, are 4 inches (10 centimetres) wide and light olive-green in colour. The sepals are fairly long, and the petals have a slightly wavy edge. The front part of the labellum is also wavy with short indentations. This variety flowers from April to March and comes from Mexico.

B. perrinii (LDL.) This variety has slender stems 6—7 inches (15—18 centimetres) long which terminate in a single narrow, tubular overhanging leaf. The blossoms form clusters of three to six flowers, and each can be up to 3 inches (8 centimetres) wide. The petals and sepals are yellow and the labellum is white. The plant blossoms from March to June and comes from Brazil.

Brassavola perrinii

Brassia

This genus comprises epiphytic orchids whose blossoms form long, one-sided clusters and in some cases short, two-sided ones. The petals and sepals of the flowers are generally elongated and pointed at the ends. The labellum is flat and somewhat short. All thirty-eight varieties comprising this genus come from tropical America. The cross-breeding of the genus *Brassia* with the genus *Oncidium* has given rise to hybrids known as *Brassidium.*

The orchids of the genus *Brassia* should be planted in soil suitable for epiphytic orchids and since they form aerial roots it is better to plant them in baskets rather than in flower-pots. In the summer months they require adequate watering, shade and humid air which is favourable for the aerial roots. In lower winter temperatures they can be watered less often and a moderately humid atmosphere is suitable for growth. The blossoms should not be left uncut too long as this tends to weaken the plants. All varieties of the genus *Brassia* grow well and flower richly. Their cultivation is no problem even for the complete beginner.

B. maculata (R. BR.) This orchid has elongated, indented stems bearing one leaf up to 14 inches (35 centimetres) long. The flower stalk can be as much as 24 inches (60 centimetres) long and bears ten to fifteen blossoms, individual flowers growing to 5½ inches (14 centimetres) across. The petals and sepals are green in colour with brown spots and the labellum is white. This variety blossoms from August to October and originates from the Antilles.

B. verrucosa (LDL.) This orchid has oval, two-leafed stems. The leaves are straight, pointed and up to 12 inches (30 centimetres) long. The flower stalk is upright 26 inches (65 centimetres) long, and bears ten to fifteen blossoms each of which is 8 inches (20 centimetres) across. The petals and sepals are narrow, pointed and light green in colour with several dark brown spots. The labellum is widely oval in shape, pointed, and is white with dark green spots. The plant blossoms from April to June and places of origin are Mexico and Guatemala.

Brassia verrucosa

Bulbophyllum

This genus also comprises epiphytic orchids with creeping roots and short stems bearing one to two leaves. A flower stalk grows from the lower side of the roots and bears one or two blossoms. About 1,000 varieties grow in Asia, Australia and South Africa.

Bulbophyllum should be transplanted before the beginning of the vegetation period and soil suitable for epiphytic orchids used. Small baskets or bowls should be chosen, but it is also possible to attach the orchids to a cork base. Some varieties can be cultivated in a hot greenhouse and others in a moderate one but during the vegetation period the plants require moist, fresh air. After the flowering period the plants require less watering, as in the winter months.

The genus *Bulbophyllum* includes a number of small morphologically interesting, varieties not requiring much space in a greenhouse or in the home, making them particularly suitable for cultivation by amateurs.

B. barbigerum (LDL.) This orchid comes from tropical Africa. It has wide oval stems, 1 inch (2·5 centimetres) long, which bear one leaf about 3 inches (7 centimetres) long and 1 inch (2·5 centimetres) wide. The cluster of blossoms is 6 inches (15 centimetres) long and bears eight to fourteen flowers, 1 inch (2·5 centimetres) across which grow in two rows and stand out horizontally. The petals and sepals are purple in colour. The labellum is about 1—2 inches (2—5 centimetres) long, strap-shaped and green with a brown pattern. Its tip is covered in fine hairs. The plant blossoms in June and July.

B. carreyanum (LDL.) This orchid comes from South Africa. It has wide oval stems 1—1½ inches (2·5—4 centimetres) long, each bearing a leaf 3 inches (8 centimetres) wide. The flower stalk is about 6 inches (15 centimetres) long and terminates in six to eight blossoms standing out horizontally each of which is 1 inch (2·5 centimetres) across. The petals and sepals of the flowers are yellowish-green with red spots. The labellum is small and reddish-brown. This orchid blossoms in December and January.

B. lobbii (LDL.) This variety comes from Java and Sumatra. The stems are subovate 2 inches (5 centimetres) long, and bear one leaf. The leaves of the plant are strap-shaped and narrow in their lower region. They are about 8 inches (20 centimetres) long and 2 inches (5 centimetres) wide. The individual blossoms, about 4 inches (10 centimetres) wide, grow in long clusters. The sepals, which stand out, are elongated and yellow with red spots on their outer side while the petals are yellow, pointed with red stripes on their outer side. The labellum is subovate and golden-yellow in colour with purple spots. The plant flowers in May and June.

Bulbophyllum carreyanum

Calanthe

This genus comprises tropical, terrestrial orchids which are divided into two groups. The first group consists of plants with thick, elongated stems with leaves which are shed every year. The flower stalk grows from the base of the roots. The second group comprises plants without stems and with non-deciduous leaves. The flower stalks grow from rosettes.

The orchids of both groups have wide leaves up to 12 inches (30 centimetres) long and a large number of blossoms with irregular petals and sepals. The labellum is quadrilobate and usually grows backwards in the form of a slender spur. About sixty varieties come mainly from tropical Asia and a small number from South Africa and Central America.

The orchids of this genus which have deciduous leaves should be transplanted every year in spring, at the beginning of the vegetation period, using soil for terrestrial orchids. Roots that are more than two years old should be separated and used for propagation. After taking root the transplanted plants should be adequately watered until the end of September and, in summer, adequately ventilated. They also require relatively large amounts of light and warmth. The leaves of the plants begin to turn yellow when the plants blossom in December, and in January they have no leaves. At the end of the blossoming period watering should cease and the plants left at a temperature of 15°C (59°F) until ready for transplanting.

Plants with non-deciduous leaves should also be cultivated in a hot greenhouse, but they require less watering even in the winter period. In summer these orchids need more shade.

C. veratrifolia (R. BR.) This variety has non-deciduous leaves, and originates from Australia and India. The flower stalk is about 40 inches (1 metre) long and rich clusters of blossoms 1½ inches (4 centimetres) wide, are snow-white in colour. The labellum is quadrilobate and its underside covered with yellow spots. The plant blossoms in April and May.

C. vestita (LDL.) This orchid comes from India. It has long, thick stems and the wide leaves fall before it begins to flower. The stalk is about 24 inches (60 centimetres) long and the petals and sepals of the blossoms are white. The labellum has yellowish-red spots. This variety of orchid blossoms from December until February.

Calanthe vestita

Catasetum

This genus comprises both epiphytic and semi-epiphytic orchids, whose blossoms are unisexual and differ greatly in appearance. The unisexual blossoms make the genus *Catasetum* very interesting from a morphological point of view. The slightest touch from an insect will cause the male flowers to scatter pollen which sticks to the insect's body, and is thus transferred to the stigmas of female flowers on subsequent visits to other blossoms. The stem roots are spindle-shaped. About 115 varieties come from tropical America.

Catasetum should be transplanted in spring just before the start of the new growth, using soil suitable for epiphytic orchids. After transplantation the plants must be watered very carefully as the newly forming buds are very sensitive to moisture. Throughout the vegetation period they should be placed in a hot greenhouse with plenty of light. When the plants are well-rooted they can be watered abundantly, but after the blossoming period they can gradually be given less. When the leaves have turned yellow, watering should stop altogether and the plants transferred to a cooler environment.

C. fimbriatum (LDL.) This variety comes from Brazil. The hanging clusters of flowers are somewhat sparse, 16 inches (40 centimetres) long and comprise seven to twenty blossoms. The individual flowers are as much as 2½ inches (7 centimetres) wide. The petals and sepals are pointed with yellowish-red spots and the labellum is yellowish. The plant blossoms in May and June.

C. macrocarpum (RICH.) This orchid comes from tropical America. The stems are fleshy and spindle-shaped with five to six thin leaves. The flower stalk is 18 inches (45 centimetres) high and bears four to ten blossoms. The latter are bell-shaped and have a diameter of 2½ inches (7 centimetres). The petals and sepals are pointed and green in colour with red spots, while the labellum is hooded and yellow. The plant flowers in October and up to December.

C. pileatum (RCHB. F.) This orchid originates from tropical America, and is the most beautiful variety of the genus. The flower stalk is about 12 inches (30 centimetres) long and bears four to eight blossoms which are 4 inches (10 centimetres) across. The petals and sepals are greyish-white and the labellum is light yellow on top and orange-red on its under side. This plant flowers in October.

Catasetum fimbriatum

Cattleya

This genus comprises tropical epiphytic orchids featuring large rootstocks and stems which can be swollen to a spindle-like shape, subovate or even tubular. The blossoms of the plants grow singly, 2—8 inches (5—20 centimetres) across or in clusters containing up to twenty flowers. Approximately forty varieties of this genus come from tropical America.

The genus *Cattleya* is botanically related to the genera *Laelia*, *Sophronitis*, *Epidendrum*, *Brassavola* and *Schomburgkia*. Hybrids obtained by cross-breeding *Cattleya* varieties with these genera flower much more easily than the original varieties, and show greater resistance to temperature changes.

The majority of the varieties forming the genus *Cattleya* thrive well in a moderate greenhouse. The non-vegetation period of numerous types falls in the autumn and winter months. During this period watering should be considerably restricted, and it is sufficient to inspect the plants once a week and to water merely those that appear dry. Spraying should also stop in the non-vegetation period. In order to ensure the required humidity in the greenhouse the pathways and tables between the flowerpots can be watered. When the plants have buds visible watering can be carried out more frequently, but only until the blossoms begin to fade, when it should be restricted again.

During the winter period all plants should be inspected and classified according to whether they are to be transplanted in spring, or merely provided with fresh surface soil. They should be planted in the soil mixture suitable for epiphytic orchids. Those varieties which blossom in autumn and winter can be transplanted in March and April, that is as soon as they begin to grow new roots, but those flowering in June should be transplanted at the end of the blossoming period. Regular annual transplantation is not necessary, and is harmful rather than beneficial. As a rule the orchid plants should be transplanted once every three years, following which the plants form only small roots and produce fewer or smaller blossoms.

Plants intended for transplantation should be removed from their flowerpots and the old soil mixture thoroughly removed. During this process it is important not to damage the healthy, white roots. The vessels in which they are to be transplanted should be chosen according to the size of the rootstock and should the latter be extensive, wooden baskets or flat bowls are the most suitable choice. If the rootstock is less extensive suitably sized flowerpots can be used.

Cattleya citrina

Fairly large pieces of pine bark can be placed in the bottom of the baskets to prevent soil from falling through and if flowerpots are used, they should be filled to one third with fine pieces of bark for drainage purposes. A small amount of soil mixture can be scattered over the bark on which the plant is placed, and the roots spread. Small quantities of soil should then be placed round the roots which can be firmed down using a wooden peg. Once transplanted, the rootstock should be at least 1 inch (2·5 centimetres) higher than the edge of the basket or flowerpot. The plants must be planted firmly in order that their newly growing roots do not break during growth in the vessels. It is recommended that a small wooden stick is placed near the plant and the new shoot bound to it.

After transplantation the orchid plants should be watered once and well, and then left dry until new roots put in an appearance. At this time, or shortly afterwards, a new stem begins to grow from the bud of the previous one. It is then that the plants should be watered more frequently and fertilized with a weak manure solution. The humidity in the greenhouse should also be increased by pouring water over the walls and paths. Care should be taken to ensure that a suitable amount of shade as well as fresh air is provided.

When the stems of the plants are well grown prolonged watering can be restricted in case new shoots are produced instead of blossoms. The amount of shade should be restricted gradually to avoid over exposure as this tends to produce black spots on the leaves, spoiling their appearance. When the buds are about half-grown watering can be restarted and continued throughout the whole blossoming period.

Cattleya orchids can be cultivated well in the home, particularly on a glass verandah that has double-glazing and adequate heating. However, the same principles should be followed as apply to their cultivation in greenhouses. Orchids of the genus *Cattleya* enjoy great popularity due to their exquisite colouring and shape.

C. amethystoglossa (LIND. and RCHB. F.) This variety comes from Brazil and is about 32 inches (80 centimetres) high with narrow, tubular stems bearing two thick leaves. The cluster of blossoms can comprise up to eight flowers which are 3 inches (8 centimetres) wide. The sepals are narrow, and the petals wide and pale pink in colour with purple spots. The labellum is wide and bluish-purple. The plant blossoms in April and May.

Cattleya horace

C. bowringiana (VEITCH.) The home of this orchid is Central America. The leaf stems grow from a wide base, can be up to 20 inches (50 centimetres) high and end in two leaves. The flower stalk bears five to ten blossoms, and individual flowers can be 3 inches (8 centimetres) across and purple in colour. The plant blossoms in October and November, grows very quickly and can easily be propagated vegetatively.

C. citrina (LDL.) Mexico is the home of this orchid and it grows in a hanging manner from the lower side of tree branches. It has subovate stems 2 inches (5 centimetres) long which bear two or three narrow, strap-shaped leaves which are greyish-green in colour. The blossoms grow singly, are lemon-yellow in colour and are tulip-shaped. They are also strongly scented and appear in October and up to April.

C. dowiana (BATEM.) This variety comes from Costa Rica and is characterized by slightly flat stems ending in a single leaf. The flower stalk is short and bears fifteen blossoms, the individual flowers being up to 6 inches (15 centimetres) across. The petals and sepals are yellow with carmine tint on their lower side. The labellum is wide and purplish-mauve in colour. This orchid blossoms from June to September.

C. horace This orchid is a hybrid obtained from *C. trianae* and *C. woltersiana* varieties. It grows to medium size, the leaf stems being up to 14 inches (35 centimetres) long and ending in a fleshy leaf. The flower sepals are narrow, the petals wide, pinkish-mauve, and wavy on their edge. The labellum is wide, reddish-mauve on the outside and lighter in the middle, and has fringed edges. The plant blossoms in September and October.

Cattleya miniscia

C. labiata (LDL.) The home of this orchid is Brazil. The leaf stems are slightly flat and end in a single leaf. The flower stalk is short with two to five flowers and individual blossoms are up to 6 inches (15 centimetres) across, their petals and sepals being mauvish-pink. The labellum has a purplish-red edge. The plant blossoms in November and December.

C. miniscia (VEITCH.) This variety of orchid comes from Central America. The leaf stems are up to 12 inches (30 centimetres) long and end in a single leaf. The flower stalk bears four to six flowers 4 inches (10 centimetres) across and rich mauvish-pink in colour. The plant flowers in November and December.

C. mossiae (HOOK.) This orchid comes from Venezuela. The stems are slender and long, ending in one thick leaf. The flowers, which are pale pink, grow in small clusters of two or three. The labellum is mauvish-purple. The plant blossoms in May and June and has many varieties.

C. percivaliana (RCHB. F.) This orchid also comes from Venezuela and in its manner of growth resembles *C. mossiae*. The flower stalk usually bears two blossoms 5½ inches (14 centimetres) across. The petals and sepals of the flowers are pale pink or lilac with a dark red tint. The labellum is orange-yellow, the front part of which is dark carmine. The plant blossoms from January to March.

C. trianae (RCHB. F.) The original home of this orchid was Colombia. The leaf stems are slightly flat and end in a single leaf. The flower stalk bears two to three blossoms which are pale pink in colour and 6—7 inches (15—18 centimetres) across. This variety grows very well in a greenhouse and blossoms in January and February.

Cattleya trianae

Chysis

The orchids of this group are epiphytic with narrow, spindle-shaped stems bearing three to five leaves on their upper halves. The flower stalk bears a cluster of three to ten blossoms. About six varieties of this genus grow in Central America.

Orchids of the genus *Chysis* should be grown in a light, moderately warm greenhouse. At the beginning of the vegetation period they should be transplanted in soil suitable for epiphytic orchids, and grow best when attached to a branch, piece of cork, or in baskets. When the plants have taken root they can be well watered and provided with a little shade. From October to spring, watering may be almost completely unnecessary. The majority of varieties blossom from March to June.

Ch. bractescens (LDL.) This orchid has narrow stems each bearing five leaves. The flower stalk is pendent with three to eight blossoms which are white in colour and 3 inches (8 centimetres) across. The labellum is white around its edges and yellow inside with red stripes and spots. The plant blossoms in March and April, and comes from Mexico.

Ch. laevis (LDL.) The home of this variety is also Mexico. It has narrow stems bearing a number of leaves and the flower clusters comprise eight to ten blossoms each of which is 3 inches (8 centimetres) wide. Their colour is yellow, the centre being shaded brown. The labellum is light yellow, with the centre striped in red. This plant blossoms in June and July.

Ch. limminghei (LIND. and RCHB. F.) This orchid comes from Mexico. The stems are very slender and bear three to five leaves. The blossoms are white with light mauve edges, and the labellum yellow on its inner part, with the front part spotted in mauve. The plant flowers in May and June.

Chysis bractescens

Cochlioda

This genus comprises epiphytic orchids and a small number of terrestrial varieties. The leaf stems are short and indented on one side. They bear one or two leaves, and the flowers are simple or ramose. About five varieties come from Peru, Ecuador and Colombia.

These orchids should be transplanted at the beginning of the vegetation period, using the soil mixture suitable for epiphytic orchids. They are cultivated under the same conditions as the genus *Odontoglossum* and consequently can be located in the same environment. During the vegetation period, however, they require more light and a higher temperature together with an abundance of fresh, moist air. In autumn, after the blossoming period and throughout the whole winter, they should be placed in a cold greenhouse and watered only rarely.

C. densiflora (LDL.) [syn. *C. noezliana* (ROLFE)] Originally from Peru, this orchid has subovate leaf stems 1—1½ inches (2·5—4 centimetres) high which bear one leaf up to 10 inches (25 centimetres) long. The flower stalk is 14 inches (35 centimetres) long with a luxuriant cluster of bright scarlet flowers. The plant blossoms from June to October. When cross-bred with various varieties of the genera *Odontoglossum*, *Oncidium*, *Miltonia*, and others, *C. densiflora* gives rise to a number of hybrids of which *Odontioda* in particular features exquisite and rich blossoms. They can be cultivated without difficulty in a cold greenhouse and provide an abundance of flowers for cutting.

C. rosea (BTH.) The home of this orchid is Peru. The flower stalk has sparse clusters up to 18 inches (45 centimetres) long. The blossoms are a dark pinkish-red and they appear in March and up to June.

C. sanguinea (BTH.) This orchid comes from Ecuador. The flower stalk branches and blossoms are pinkish-red with a white labellum. The plant flowers from October to November.

Cochlioda densiflora

Coelogyne

This genus comprises epiphytic and terrestrial orchids which came originally from the monsoon areas, namely from Ceylon to the Samoan Islands. About 150 varieties are included in this genus.

The leaf stems of the individual varieties are short and of varied shapes, rounded or elongated, one- or two-leaved, and are ever-green. The blossoms grow in clusters, and the petals and sepals are very similar, that is, bent in an arch-like manner. The labellum is concave and small. Depending on the particular variety, the blossoms develop either simultaneously or successively. Only some types are suitable for cultivation as the majority have unattractive flowers which tend to wither rapidly.

The most suitable time for planting *Coelogyne* orchids is when they begin to form new roots, and soil suitable for epiphytic orchids should be used. However, with *C. cristata* variety some humus should be added. Wide, shallow bowls or baskets are recommended rather than flowerpots, as these plants grow sideways. Annual transplantation is not desirable, and it is sufficient merely to remove old, dead roots and to fill the resulting gaps with fresh soil. During the vegetation period the plants require fresh, warm air and a light amount of shade. By the end of August the newly grown roots are well developed and consequently moderate watering is advisable. The plants should also be ventilated more frequently and allowed to become accustomed to light. In the winter period the plants should be kept under drier conditions at a temperature of 12—15°C (54—59°F). When flower-buds begin to appear watering can be carried out more frequently.

When cultivated in the home these plants should be placed near a window where sufficient light is guaranteed. In the summer months the window should be lightly covered with a curtain to reduce the effect of the mid-day sun.

Coelogyne cristata

C. asperata (LDL.) This is an epiphytic orchid which originally came from Borneo. The stems are wide and long and bear two elongated, elliptic leaves. The creamy white flowers grow in hanging clusters of seven to ten flowers. They can be up to 3½ inches (9 centimetres) across and blossom in June and July.

C. cristata (LDL.) This orchid comes from the Himalayas. The rounded leaf stems end in patterned leaves 10 inches (25 centimetres) long and 1 inch (2·5 centimetres) wide. The flowers grow in clusters comprising five to nine blossoms which are 3—4 inches (8—10 centimetres) wide, snow-white in colour and with five yellow crests on their labellum. They flower in January and up to March.

C. dayana (RCHB. F.) The home of this variety is Borneo. The leaf stems are narrow and subovate with two narrow leaves. The flower stalk is pendent, up to 40 inches (1 metre) long and bearing many blossoms snow-white in colour and 2½ inches (7 centimetres) across. The labellum is brown with six white spots. This plant blossoms from April to June.

C. massangeana (RCHB. F.) This orchid comes from Java and Borneo. The leaf stems are subovate and 4 inches (10 centimetres) long. The leaves are relatively large and of a narrow elliptic shape. The blossoms grow in hanging clusters which are up to 20 inches (50 centimetres) long with fifteen to twenty flowers. The latter are creamy yellow in colour with a brown-edged labellum. The plant blossoms in June and July.

Coelogyne massangeana

Cymbidium

This genus is represented by epiphytic and terrestrial orchids possessing a short stalk twisted into a flat stem with numerous patterned, leathery leaves. The blossoms grow in clusters and the petals and sepals are similar in appearance. The labellum stands out and is trilobate. About fifty varieties come from tropical and sub-tropical Africa, Asia and Australia.

A spacious greenhouse with good ventilation is necessary for the cultivation of these orchids as they need an abundance of fresh air. It is recommended that the vessels containing the orchids are placed in peat or green *Sphagnum* as the roots should not be exposed to any great warmth.

The orchids of this genus should be transplanted after a few years and should be carried out after the blossoming period in spring, using soil suitable for terrestrial orchids. The growing period of the plants is from March to August during which time they require frequent watering, moderate shade and the weekly addition of a nutrient solution. This should consist of a weak manure solution and a solution of inorganic nutrients (described in the introduction) used alternately. By the end of August most of the plants have well developed shoots, and should therefore be removed to a dry environment. The sooner the shoots are developed and the sooner watering is stopped the better the blossom appears in spring.

In autumn the orchids should be kept dry at a temperature of 10—12°C (50—54°F) and hardly watered at all until the flower stalks begin to grow. The whole flowerpot should then be submerged in water and the plants transferred to a warmer environment once again. The flower stalks then grow to a length of as much as 40 inches (1 metre) and bear fifteen to twenty blossoms. The colouring of the flowers can be enhanced by artificial lighting. Strong plants grow a number of stalks and in the absence of the dry and cool period, leafy shoots often appear instead of blossoms.

Even when orchids of the genus *Cymbidium* are cultivated in the home, the conditions applying during their vegetation period can easily be observed. In the summer months the plants can be placed near an open window or, better still, on a balcony or in the garden under a tree offering moderate shade. The conditions of the non-vegetation period must also be observed when these orchids are cultivated in the home.

Cymbidium adrian

C. adrian This orchid is a hybrid of medium growth, and results from the cross-breeding of *C. viceroy* and *C. swallow*. The leaves are 1 inch (2·5 centimetres wide) and up to 32 inches (80 centimetres) long. The flower stalks are pendent and bear twelve to eighteen flowers 3—4 inches (8—10 centimetres) wide. The petals and sepals are white in colour with a pink tint and the labellum is white with red spots.

C. giganteum (WALL.) This variety originally came from the Himalayas. The patterned leaves can be up to 26 inches (65 centimetres) long, and the scented blossoms up to 4 inches (10 centimetres) across. The sepals and petals are yellowish-green in colour with brown stripes. The labellum is yellow and trilobate. The plant blossoms in September and October.

C. insigne (ROLFE.) The home of this orchid is Vietnam. The leaves are 20—36 inches (50—90 centimetres) long and 1 inch (2·5 centimetres) wide. The flower stalk can be as much as 4 feet (1·2 metres) high and bears ten to fifteen blossoms which stand out from the stalk and are 3½ inches (9 centimetres) across. The petals and sepals are light pink in colour, the labellum trilobate and pinkish-red with purple spots. The plant blossoms from March to May.

C. lowianum (RCHB. F.) This plant comes from Burma. The leaves are up to 30 inches (75 centimetres) long and end in points. The flower stalks are pendent and bear ten to twenty blossoms, which can be up to 4 inches (10 centimetres) across and are very durable. The sepals and petals are greenish-yellow in colour. The labellum is trilobate and yellow, with the front part bright scarlet. The plant blossoms in February and up to June.

C. nicolasianum. This orchid is a hybrid resulting from the cross-breeding of *C. hanburyanum*, *C. pearl* and *C. swallow*. It is a large plant with leaves up to 1 inch (2·5 centimetres) wide and 30 inches (75 centimetres) long. The flower stalks bear twelve to fifteen blossoms 4 inches (10 centimetres) wide. The petals and sepals are reddish-brown, and the labellum is darker in the centre and lighter on its edges. The plant blossoms in January and February.

Cymbidium nicolasianum

Dendrobium

The orchids of this genus are epiphytic. About 1,000 varieties are widespread in the tropics and sub-tropics, namely from Ceylon to the Samoan Islands. Some grow to the north of Japan, others in New Zealand. The plants have segmented stems, some quite short and twisted while others are slender and tubular. The leaves can be deciduous or non-deciduous, and grow in two rows or in a spiral fashion up the stem. The blossoms of this orchid grow singly in rare cases, and more often in clusters at the end of the stalk.

The period of growth of these plants is from March to August and those which thrive in a warm atmosphere, such as *D. phalaenopsis*, begin to vegetate as early as May. The most suitable time for transplanting is shortly before the growth of new roots, i.e. in March. Large plants can be planted in wooden baskets and smaller ones in flowerpots. They also grow well when attached to bark and established in a soil mixture suitable for epiphytic orchids. Once planted, the orchids should be watered well, after which watering should be restricted until new roots appear. During the vegetation period watering should be carried out more frequently and the whole plant sprayed.

Dendrobiums are less sensitive to the heat of the sun than other orchids and consequently they require protection only when the sun's rays become more intense, i.e. at the beginning of May. During this period they also need a high degree of moisture and a warm environment and attention should also be paid to their fertilization. Apart from the roots, the leaves should also be sprayed, and for this purpose a weak manure solution or one made up of inorganic nutrients can be used. Fertilization of the leaves should be carried out after sunset so that the plants may absorb the solution well. Fertilization by fumigation can also be carried out by placing solutions of organic nutrients under the tables of the greenhouse.

Watering, spraying and fertilization should be carried out until the shoots are well developed, indicated by examination of their tips. The leaves of these plants grow opposite one another on the stems and should a single leaf appear at the top of a stem, it means that the period of growth has ended and watering and spraying can be carried out minimally. In addition, the plants need no longer be shaded, but need to be well ventilated. The shoots ripen in the sun and become hard. In the case of some deciduous varieties leaves on two-year old shoots turn yellow and drop off, whereupon the plants should be moved to a light place in a cold, dry and airy greenhouse. This procedure is essential for flowering, and corresponds to the natural climatic conditions which exist in their original home. If Dendrobiums are left in a warm dry greenhouse young plants often grow on the flower stalks instead of blossoms.

Dendrobium finlayanum

When Dendrobiums are placed in a cool and dry environment small round bodies begin to appear on the stems, and these are termed embryo blossoms. If the plants are required to flower at Christmas time, they must be moved to a warm greenhouse six weeks beforehand and watered. Frequent watering in this period ensures the growth of blossoms as well as their correct colouring. If the plants are required to blossom successively, those with developed buds should be moved in sequence from the cold greenhouse to a hot one, as this procedure ensures flowering plants throughout the whole winter period.

Dendrobiums can be ranked among the orchids which thrive well in home conditions. During the vegetation period they require warmth and moisture, and consequently, after transplantation in spring, they should be placed in glass show-cases, glass window boxes or even large 'terraria'. They should be planted in small baskets, flowerpots or attached to cork and it is important that they are placed in a sunny place.

When cultivated in the home Dendrobiums need not be shaded as they are not exposed to enough sunshine to harm them. Should cold days occur during the vegetation period, the room in which they are placed should be adequately heated. If a single leaf appears on the new shoots (in the case of deciduous varieties) the plants should be placed in a window to ensure exposure to full sunshine, and watering can be gradually restricted until it is stopped completely. When buds begin to appear after leaf fall the plants may be moved to a warm environment and watering recommenced. Non-deciduous Dendrobiums such as *D. phalaenopsis* and other varieties, should be kept in a warm environment throughout the whole year. In winter they can be watered less frequently.

D. chrysanthum (WALL.) The home of this plant is also the Himalayas. The stalks are fleshy and up to 60 inches (1·5 metres) long, and are entirely covered with elongated, pointed, deciduous leaves. The blossoms are waxy and grow in twos or threes. They are about 1½ inches (4 centimetres) wide and gold-yellow in colour with a frayed labellum. The plant usually blossoms in August and September.

D. chrysotoxum (LDL.) This orchid originally came from Burma. The leaf stems end in two to six elongated, leathery, non-deciduous leaves. The blossoms grow in pendent clusters comprising eight to fifteen flowers which are up to 2 inches (5 centimetres) across. They are golden-yellow in colour with an orange labellum having a fringed edge. This plant blossoms from November to April.

Dendrobium moschatum

D. crassinode (RCHB.) This orchid originally came from the Himalayas and has most beautiful, large blossoms. The flower stalks are relatively thick with intersegments. The blossoms grow in threes along the whole length of the stalks. They are pink in colour with a round, carmine labellum.

D. devonianum (LDL.) This plant comes from the Himalayas. It has very slender, pendent stems up to 32 inches (80 centimetres) long with deciduous leaves. The blossoms grow on the upper third of the stalk, either singly or in twos, and are 2 inches (5 centimetres) across. The petals and sepals are white in colour with dark purple tips while the labellum is white with two orange spots. This orchid blossoms in May and June.

D. fimbriatum (HOOK.) The home of this orchid is Himalayas. The flower stalks are up to 48 inches (1·2 metres) high and end in wide leaves. The blossoms grow in pendent clusters of eight to fifteen flowers and are light orange in colour and 2 inches (5 centimetres) wide. The labellum is light yellow and fringed. This orchid blossoms in March to May.

D. finlayanum (PAR. and RCHB. F.) This orchid has leaf stems up to 20 inches (50 centimetres) long, and its leaves are ½ inch (1 centimetre) wide and pointed. The blossoms usually grow in pairs on flower stems arising from the main stalk. The petals and sepals are light mauve and the labellum is oval in shape with a golden-yellow centre with white edges. The plant blossoms in February and March and comes from Burma.

D. moschatum (SW.) The home of this orchid is the Himalayas. It has tubular stems which are fleshy and have lanceolate leaves. The blossoms grow on two year old stalks, forming sparse clusters of seven to fifteen flowers. The individual blossoms are 3 inches (8 centimetres) across. The petals and sepals are honey gold in colour and the labellum is shoe-shaped with two dark brownish-red spots. This plant flowers in June.

D. nobile (LDL.) This orchid also comes from the Himalayas. It has fleshy, segmented stems with lanceolate leaves which appear after two years. The blossoms grow on two-year old stalks after the leaves have fallen, and are pinkish-purple in colour with a white, pink edged labellum having a purple spot at its mouth. This orchid is a most widely spread variety and blossoms from December to April.

Dendrobium nobile var. *sanderianum*

D. nobile var. *sanderianum.* This plant has fleshy, segmented stems which are much thicker and longer than those of the original *D. nobile.* The leaves remain on the plant for two years and the blossoms grow on two year old stalks in pairs. The individual flowers are up to 3 inches (8 centimetres) across, pinkish-purple in colour and blossom from January to April.

D. phalaenopsis (FITZG.) The home of this orchid is New Guinea. It has a fleshy, segmented stalk up to 28 inches (70 centimetres) high and leathery, lanceolate leaves which remain on the plant for a number of years. The blossoms are cherry-red with a darker labellum, characterized by a purple mouth and a short spur. The flower stems grow from the same spots for a number of years. This plant is most valuable as regards the suitability of its blooms for cutting.

D. pierardii (ROXB.) Originating from the Himalayas, this deciduous plant has slender hanging leaf stems which can reach a length of 36 inches (90 centimetres). The leaves are elongated and pointed. The blooms grow in twos or threes on a single stalk and the petals and sepals are pink in colour and transparent, while the labellum is yellow with red veins. The plant flowers from April to May.

D. superbiens (RCHB. F.) This orchid comes from northern Australia, and its flowers grow at the end of the stalks. Each cluster has fifteen to twenty-five blossoms which can be up to 2 inches (5 centimetres) across. The petals and sepals are slightly wavy in appearance and are pinkish-red in colour. The labellum is dark purple with white crests. This variety is very suitable for cutting and should be kept in a warm environment throughout the whole year. The blossoming period is in March and April.

Dendrobium phalaenopsis

Epidendrum

The orchids of this genus are epiphytic and are characterized by highly varied forms. Some have stems, while others have a leafy, segmented stalk bearing elongated, leathery leaves. The blooms grow mainly in clusters which are sometimes compact and sometimes branched. Approximately 800 varieties grow in tropical America, from Florida to Paraguay.

Most of the varieties of this genus should be cultivated in a moderate greenhouse, as with the genus *Cattleya*. The plants should be transplanted in spring when they begin to form new roots and soil for epiphytic orchids used. During the summer months they require an adequate amount of fresh but not too warm air, and moderate shade. In the winter period watering should be carried out only rarely but those varieties which do not produce stems can be watered more often.

E. prismatocarpum (RCHB. F.) The home of this orchid is Costa Rica. It has slender leaf stems which are subovate, 6 inches (15 centimetres) high, and bear two to three leaves. The flower stalk is about 16 inches (40 centimetres) long and bears a large number of blooms. These are 1½—2 inches (4—5 centimetres) across, bright yellow in colour with brown spots. The labellum is pinkish-red. This orchid blossoms from May to July.

E. stamfordianum (BATEM.) Coming from Guatemala, this orchid has rounded stems up to 6½ inches (16 centimetres) long with three to four elongated leaves. The flower stalk can be up to 16 inches (40 centimetres) wide and strongly scented. The labellum is white in colour with yellowish edges. The plant flowers in March and April.

E. vitellinum (LDL.) This variety requires a cold greenhouse, and is highly suitable for cutting. It has short, subovate stems bearing two to three large bluish-green leaves. The clusters of flowers grow in an upright manner and the blossoms number ten to twenty in each cluster. They are 1½ inches (4 centimetres) wide and a bright orange-red in colour. The labellum is golden-yellow. This plant blossoms from October to December, and originates from Mexico.

Epidendrum vitellinum

Laelia

This genus comprises epiphytic tropical orchids related to those of the genus *Cattleya*. The blooms are large with a conspicuous, cornet-shaped, usually simple labellum. Most of them have long, fleshy stems bearing one, or sometimes two leaves at their tip. The home of this genus is tropical America, from Mexico to Brazil.

The majority of the varieties comprised in this group can be cultivated in a moderate greenhouse, as with orchids of the genus *Cattleya*. Some varieties, such as *L. pumila*, can be grown well in the home. The plants should be transplanted in soil suitable for epiphytic orchids, and ideally in baskets. These can be hung near glass and lightly shaded. At the height of the vegetation period the orchids should be frequently watered and sprayed, but in the non-vegetation months they require far less moisture than other varieties. As long as the blossoms remain on the plants they flower for a long time, but they fade very soon after cutting. The cross-breeding of orchids of the genus *Laelia* with varieties of *Cattleya* has given rise to hybrids known as *Laeliocattleya*.

L. crispa (RCHB. F.) This orchid comes from Brazil. The leaf stems are slender and compressed, bearing one strap-shaped leaf. The flower stalk can be up to 14 inches (35 centimetres) long and bears four to seven blooms 5 inches (12 centimetres) across. The petals and sepals are white, the labellum trilobate and white, with the inner part yellow with red veins. The plant blossoms from June to August.

L. gouldiana (RCHB. F.) The home of this plant is Mexico. The leaf stems are long, oval and bear two leaves. The flower stalk can be 18 inches (45 centimetres) long and bears three to six blossoms about 4 inches (10 centimetres) across. The sepals are narrow, and the petals wide and dark pinkish-red in colour. The labellum is trilobate and dark reddish-mauve with yellow veins. The plant flowers in December and January.

Laelia gouldiana

L. harpophylla (RCHB. F.) This plant has slender, tubular stems with one very narrow leaf up to 8 inches (20 centimetres) long. The flower stalk is slender and bears three to six blooms 2 inches (5 centimetres) across. They are orange in colour and flower from March to May. The home of this orchid is Brazil.

L. pumila (RCHB. F.) Originating from Brazil, this orchid is characterized by its sparse growth. The leaf stems are short and have only one leaf, blossoms grow singly and are about 4 inches (10 centimetres) wide. The petals and sepals are a bright mauvish-pink and the labellum is dark mauve with two light spots. This plant flowers in September and October.

L. purpurata (LDL.) This orchid also comes from Brazil. The leaf stems are long and slender, tubular in shape with one strap-shaped leaf. The flower stalk is short and bears three to five blooms 6½—7 inches (16—18 centimetres) across. The petals and sepals are light pink in colour, the labellum funnel-shaped and dark red with a dark, wavy edge. *Laelia* produces the largest blossoms of the varieties in this genus and the flowering period lasts from May to July.

Laelia harpophylla

Lycaste

The orchids comprising this genus are epiphytic varieties although a few are terrestrial. The stems are subovate, flattened and bear one or more leaves. The blossoms grow singly from the base of the stalks on short stems bearing a number of scaly leaves. They are fairly large with bent petals and sepals, while the labellum is small. About thirty-five varieties grow in tropical and subtropical America.

This genus of orchids is more popular in the home since the blossoms have short stems and are not suitable for cutting. Each plant usually produces five to six blooms. After the blossoming period the plants should be transplanted in terrestrial orchid soil with an addition of chopped beech leaves. Once transplanted, they should be placed in an ambient temperature of 15—16°C (59—61°F). In March new shoots begin to appear, often on older stems while leaves on the old stems die, until only on the newly grown ones remain. During the vegetation period, provided the plants are well-rooted, fairly frequent watering with a weak manure solution is beneficial.

After completion of growth and the development of leaf stems, when the majority of the leaves fall, watering should be carried out only to prevent the plants from drying up. During this period they can be placed in a light and cool environment and only when buds appear should watering recommence.

Lycaste aromatica

L. aromatica (LDL.) The home of this orchid is Mexico. The flowers are light orange in colour with a strong scent of cinnamon. It blooms in April and May.

L. cruenta (LDL.) The blooms of this orchid are dark orange in colour with a red-spotted base, and can be up to 3½ inches (9 centimetres) wide. They flower in March, and the plant originates from Guatemala.

L. skinneri (LDL.) The home of this orchid is Mexico. It produces large flowers up to 6 inches (15 centimetres) wide with pinkish sepals and dark pink to reddish petals. The labellum is trilobate and its front lobe yellow with red spots. The plant blossoms from October to December.

Lycaste skinneri

Masdevallia

These orchids are epiphytic and bear narrow leaves without stems. The blossoms grow from the axils of the leaves, either singly or in clusters. The sepals are relatively large, wide at the base and elongated at the tip with narrow appendages. The petals are always smaller and narrow and the labellum small and strap or mussel-shaped. Approximately 150 varieties grow in tropical Central and South America.

The orchids of this genus thrive in a cool environment and particularly in damp mountain regions. Consequently they should be cultivated in a cold greenhouse or in a northerly facing room in the home. The orchids should be transplanted either at the end of January or in September, using epiphytic orchid soil in flat bowls. However, *M. bella* and *M. chimaera* varieties are more usually transplanted in baskets since their flower stalks grow sideways. The orchids of this genus love fresh air and a high degree of humidity and shade. They should be watered moderately throughout the whole winter period.

M. bella (RCHB. F.) This plant produces large yellow blooms with extraordinarily long appendages and a white labellum. It blossoms in December.

M. caudata (LDL.) The petals of this orchid are brownish-yellow in colour while the sepals are mauve with long appendages and a pink-spotted labellum. It flowers from November to March.

M. chimaera (RCHB. F.) This plant has leaves up to 1 inch (2·5 centimetres) wide and 10 inches (25 centimetres) long. The large blossoms form an 8 inch (20 centimetres) long spur, and are dark brown in colours with light spots. The labellum is slipper-shaped and light brown. The orchid flowers from November to February.

M. coccinea (LIND.) The large flowers of this plant are mauvish-red and the labellum light pink with a white tip. The orchid blooms in March and May. All the mentioned varieties come from Colombia.

Masdevallia chimaera

Maxillaria

These are tropical epiphytic orchids of diverse appearance and have small oval leaf stems which grow from a creeping stalk. Some varieties have a large number of such stems while others only a small number. The predominant front petals of the blossoms are elongated and the labellum is trilobate in the majority of cases. About 250 varieties of this genus come from tropical America.

The genus *Maxillaria* is very interesting from the botanical viewpoint and particularly suitable for cultivation by amateur orchid growers. When planning their cultivation attention must be paid to the place of origin of the given variety and a warm, moderate or cool environment chosen accordingly.

The plants should be transplanted after the blossoming period in most cases, as this is the time when a new shoot begins to grow. Old roots and stems should be removed. Soil suitable for epiphytic orchids should be used and watering started only when new roots begin to appear. During the summer months the orchids can be provided with shade and a moist, warm and fresh atmosphere maintained. They should be watered carefully also in winter as this is the vegetation period of the genus. The larger the shoots of the plant the less watering they need.

M. grandiflora (LDL.) The home of this orchid is Ecuador. The leaf stems are oval and up to 2½ inches (7 centimetres) high, ending in a single strap-shaped leaf 14 inches (35 centimetres) long. The flower stalk is 4 inches (10 centimetres) high with one large blossom. The petals and sepals of the latter are milk-white and the labellum is wide and oval, with wine-red side lobes and a yellow front lobe. The plant blooms from May to June.

M. venusta (LDL.) This plant comes from New Granada. The leaf stems are rounded and slightly flattened. They grow 1½—2 inches (4—5 centimetres) high and have one strap-shaped leaf 12 inches (30 centimetres) long. The flower stalks grow in an upright manner and bear flowers up to 6 inches (15 centimetres) across. The sepals are longer than the petals and both are pointed and milk-white in colour. The labellum is fleshy and yellow with a red border. The plant flowers from September to November.

Maxillaria venusta

Miltonia

This genus comprises epiphytic orchids with short leaf stems ending in one to three leaves. The blossoms are large and grow either singly or in clusters. About twenty varieties are very widespread in Brazil and Colombia.

Brazilian varieties such as *M. anceps*, *M. candida* and *M. clowesii* should be cultivated in a moderate environment (see the genus *Cattleya*). Colombian varieties such as *M. phalaenopsis* and *M. vexillaria* require conversely a cold environment (see the genus *Odontoglossum*). These orchids should always be transplanted at the beginning of the vegetation period when they begin to grow new roots in soil suitable for epiphytic orchids. When the plants have taken root they should be watered well, although less frequently during the winter. During the flowering period the plants must not be sprayed as this causes dark spots to appear on the blossoms. The blooms remain on the plants for a fairly long time, but fade only a few hours after cutting.

M. candida (LDL.) The home of this orchid is Brazil. The leaf stems are narrow and subovate with two long leaves up to 12 inches (30 centimetres) long. The flower stalk can be 20 inches (50 centimetres) high and bears three to five blooms $3\frac{1}{2}$ inches (9 centimetres) across. The petals and sepals are yellow in colour and spotted in brown on their inner side. The labellum is wide and oval, and is white with a wavy border with two dark mauve spots. The plant flowers from August to November.

M. phalaenopsis (NICHOLS) This plant comes from Colombia. The oval leaf stems are compressed at the sides, and are light green in colour. They bear one or two leaves. The flower stalk is slender bearing two to four blooms $2\frac{1}{2}$ inches (6 centimetres) across. The petals and sepals are white and the labellum is dark red in the lower part with white edges. This plant blooms from August to November.

M. spectabilis (LDL.) The home of this plant is Brazil. The leaf stems are oval and grow on a creeping stalk. They are somewhat flattened and grow to a height of 3 inches (8 centimetres), bearing two leaves which are narrow, strap-shaped and up to 6 inches (15 centimetres) long. The flower stalk grows among the leaves and ends in a single, flat blossom up to 3 inches (8 centimetres) across. The petals and sepals of the flower are white or milky white with a pink tint on their lower side. The labellum is white and oval, and is wine red in colour with white or light pink edges. The orchid flowers in August.

Miltonia spectabilis

Odontoglossum

These orchids are epiphytic with subovate, partly subovate or pear-shaped leaf stems with flattened sides, and one or more leaves at their tips. The inflorescence is either upright or has the form of a panicle or cluster and the blossoms have a conspicuously wide labellum. About ninety varieties grow in the higher regions of tropical America.

The genus *Odontoglossum* comprises orchids suitable for cultivation in a cold greenhouse. In order to secure a supply of cooler air in the hot summer months it is recommended that the greenhouse is built in the vicinity of large trees. These orchids should be planted in epiphytic orchid soil with a small addition of *Sphagnum*. Small flowerpots should be used for transplantation, and at least one half filled with drainage chips and the new, young shoots placed in the centre. For a period of about three weeks the plants should be kept dry until the appearance of new roots, and then watering and spraying carried out in accordance with the weather.

In the summer months the plants should be well shaded as the ambient temperature should not exceed 20°C (68°F). Fertilization is not necessary, as the beech leaf contained in the soil mixture provides the plants with sufficient nutrients. By the end of July some varieties have already well-developed stems and consequently watering can be restricted. Shading should continue, however, until October.

The majority of varieties of this genus blossom in November, December and January and as soon as the flower stalk appears the temperature can be slightly increased, and light watering started. The flower stalk grows somewhat slowly, and it is usually six weeks before the first blooms open. The blossoms should not be left too long on the plants after their full-bloom period as they then begin to weaken the plant. The genus *Odontoglossum* provides a number of exquisite hybrids some of which blossom twice a year.

Odontoglossum grande

Odontoglossum - *continued*

O. cirrhosum (LDL.) The original home of this orchid was Ecuador. The leaf stems are narrow and subovate, reaching a height of 3 inches (8 centimetres) and bearing two leaves 12 inches (30 centimetres) long. The hanging flower stalk is up to 24 inches (60 centimetres) long and bears a large number of flowers 4—4½ inches (10—12 centimetres) wide. The petals and sepals are milky white in colour with brownish-red spots and the labellum is white and similarly spotted. This plant blossoms in April and May.

O. citrosmum (LDL.) This orchid originally came from Mexico. The petals and sepals of the blossoms are white with a faint pink tint, and the labellum is wide and kidney-shaped, pink in colour. The flowers grow in clusters on a hanging stalk and smell strongly of lemons. They blossom in May and June.

O. crispum (LDL.) The home of this plant is Colombia. It bears clusters of white flowers each with a red spotted labellum whose centre is yellow. It blossoms in February and March. A number of beautiful hybrids have been bred from this variety.

O. grande (LDL.) Originally from Guatemala, this orchid has large blossoms more than 4 inches (10 centimetres) across. They grow in sparse clusters and are yellow in colour with brown spots. The plant flowers from October to December.

O. insleayi (BARKER.) This orchid comes from Mexico. The flowers are yellow with brown spots and are 3 inches (8 centimetres) wide. They grow in an open cluster on an upright stalk, and appear from November to January.

Odontoglossum insleayi

Oncidium

The orchids of this genus are epiphytic most of them having short, flat leaf stems. The blossoms feature a conspicuously flat labellum and grow in clusters. Approximately 530 varieties grow in the tropics from Mexico through the West Indies to Bolivia and Paraguay. Although the genus *Oncidium* is very abundant, it offers a relatively small selection for cultivation.

Oncidiums should be cultivated in a cold, moderate or warm environment according to their place of origin. The majority of varieties, however, thrive in a moderate environment. Those suitable for growing in a cold greenhouse are *O. cheirophorum*, *O. cuculatum*, *O. incurvum*, *O. phalaenopsis* and *O. superbiens*; *O. ampliatum*, *O. kramerianum* and *O. papilio* are cultivated in a warm environment. All other varieties should be grown in a moderate greenhouse. Oncidiums should be transplanted in spring when new buds and roots begin to grow, and soil suitable for epiphytic orchids used. The best choice of vessels are wide bowls or baskets. During the vegetation period a high degree of humidity should be maintained and for tropical varieties a high temperature and adequate shade provided. In winter the plants should be watered merely to prevent the stems and leaves from drying up. *O. kramerianum* and *O. papilio* always produce new blossoms on old flower stalks and consequently the latter should not be cut prematurely.

C. cavendishianum (BATEM.) This orchid comes from Guatemala and Mexico. It has one wide, fleshy leaf up to 12 inches (30 centimetres) long but no stem. The flower stalk is long with branching inflorescences. The blossoms are 1½ inches (4 centimetres) across and yellow in colour with brownish-red spots. The labellum is golden-yellow with red spots. The plant flowers in April and May.

O. crispum (LODD.) Brazil is the home of this plant whose stems are subovate with two to three narrow, pointed leaves 8 inches (20 centimetres) long. The flower stalks are up to 36 inches (90 centimetres) high and bear a large number of flowers measuring 2—2½ inches (5—7 centimetres) across. The sepals are light brown with several yellow spots and the petals are of the same colour, but wider. The labellum is short and brown with yellow stripes. The plant blossoms from September to December.

Oncidium splendidum

O. incurvum (BARKER.) The home of this plant is Mexico. The oval leaf stems bear two to three narrow leaves. The flower stalk can be up to 60 inches (1·5 metres) long with extensively branched inflorescences. The strongly scented blossoms of this plant are 1 inch (2·5 centimetres) wide, and the petals and sepals white with pinkish-mauve spots. The labellum is violin-shaped, and is white with spots. This orchid flowers in September and up to November.

O. kramerianum (RCHB. F.) This orchid comes from Ecuador. The leaf stems are rounded and slightly flattened, and bear one elliptic, dark green leaf marble-patterned in blackish-green. The flower stalk is upright and reaches a height of 30 inches (75 centimetres). The blossoms resemble butterflies and flower successively. The labellum is violin-shaped and canary yellow, with its lower part dark red. The plant flowers from August to November.

O. papilio (LDL.) Venezuela is the home of this orchid which has oval leaf stems bearing fairly long, reddish leaves. The flower stalk is 24—44 inches (60—110 centimetres) high. The blossoms flower successively, are 5 inches (12 centimetres) across and reddish-brown in colour with yellow spots. The labellum is brown with a large, lemon-coloured spot. This orchid blooms throughout the whole year.

O. splendidum (A. RICH.) This plant comes from Guatemala. The leaf stems are short with one fleshy leaf. The flower stalk bears nine to twenty blossoms which are yellowish-green with dark brown spots and smell of violets. The labellum is golden-yellow with two brown spots. The plant blooms in October and to December.

O. varicosum (LDL.) Originally from Brazil, this plant has elongated leaf stems with branching leaves. The flower stalk is upright with a branching inflorescence. The blossoms, many in number, are 2—2½ inches (5—7 centimetres) wide, golden-yellow in colour with reddish-brown spots. The labellum is also golden-yellow. This orchid blooms from October to January.

Oncidium varicosum

Paphiopedilum

Paphiopedilums are ever-green plants. The leaves are thick in texture and frequently bluish in colour. The blooms are large, usually growing singly on the stalk and having a pouched, slipper-shaped labellum. These orchids have no nutritive organs either above or below ground and consequently require considerable moisture even during the non-vegetation period. The genus *Paphiopedilum* is frequently incorrectly called the genus *Cypripedium* by orchid-growers, being the name of a plant which grows in Central Europe.

The genus *Paphiopedilum* comprises about fifty varieties originating from the tropics of Indo-Malaya from the Spice Isles to New Guinea. The outstanding features of these orchids are the beautiful shape of their flowers and their durability, for example, when cut, the blossoms survive in water for four to five weeks. The orchids of this genus can be divided into three groups according to their winter temperature requirements: —

a) winter temperature: *P. insigne* and varieties.
   7—10°C (45—50°F)

b) winter temperature: *P. venustum*, *P. villosum*, *P. leanum*, *P. lathanianum*,
   12—16°C (54—61°F) *P. harrisianum*, and others.

c) winter temperature: *P. callosum*, *P. lawrenceanum*, *P. ciliolare*, *P. maudiae*,
   20—22°C (68—72°F) *P. curtisii* and others.

These temperatures should be ensured for the given varieties by amateur orchid growers as a knowledge of the temperature requirements and maintenance of the non-vegetation period of the individual orchids is essential. If these conditions are not adhered to the plants rarely blossom. The orchids in groups a) and b) should be watered less frequently after the appearance of new shoots, and the ambient temperature lowered. Paphiopedilums comprised in group c) require a high temperature in winter because they do not have a non-vegetation period. With these varieties, every fully developed shoot produces blossoms.

Paphiopedilums thrive best in small greenhouses and particularly if it is possible to devote the entire greenhouse to them. In a full greenhouse the symbiotic fungus multiplies and is thus of great benefit to the plants. They grow well if placed on tables on upturned flowerpots, but the pots should not stand too close to one another as this prevents a sufficient flow of air. During the vegetation period the orchids require moist, warm fresh air. The required humidity can be obtained by watering the pathways in the greenhouse as well as the walls and, in particular, the tables between the individual plants.

Paphiopedilum fairieanum

Those varieties which prefer a cold atmosphere should be planted in the soil mixture suitable for terrestrial orchids. Some types however, such as *P. niveum* and *P. godefroyae*, require the addition of plaster to the mixture. Warmth-loving plants, on the other hand, should be planted in the epiphytic soil mixture without any additions. These orchids can be transplanted at any time of the year, but the most suitable time for the other varieties is spring, after blooming of the flowers, and by the end of April at the latest. The size of the flowerpots should be chosen according to the size of the individual plants, and small baskets, whose size can be adapted to the growth of the plants, have proved very suitable.

Healthy, well-grown plants should have larger vessels as such specimens have a large number of roots, but should be transplanted only after three or even four years. Weak or divided plants can be planted in small flowerpots in which they take root rapidly. Before planting the orchids, the flowerpots should be filled to one third with shredded pine bark for drainage purposes, and care taken to ensure that every flowerpot is provided with a hole in its base for the same reason. Before transplanting, old soil and dead leaves must be completely removed from every plant. The drainage material should be covered with a small amount of soil before setting the plant. To ensure that the spaces between the roots are filled, a wooden peg can be used to firm the soil into the pot. The plant should be placed fairly high so that the centre of the orchid is about 1 inch (2·5 centimetres) above the edge of the flowerpot or basket. In the case of warmth-loving varieties it is recommended that the surface of the soil is covered with green *Sphagnum*, and that this is renewed two or three times a year. The presence of fresh moss encourages the growth of new roots.

After they have been transplanted the plants should not be watered too heavily or frequently to prevent damaged roots from rotting, but sprayed several times daily. If the plants are transplanted at the beginning of April they need be shaded only slightly until the beginning of May, after which more intensive shade is required. After new roots have appeared watering should be carried out normally. The plants should be well aired by means of low placed ventilators and it is also advisable at this time to fertilize the plants once a week with a weak manure solution. This procedure can be stopped at the end of August. The roots of the plants, which up to this time have had yellowish-white, sticky tips, now become covered with a brown, leathery coating.

In September it is sufficient to spray the orchids once daily during the sunny period, shading can be removed gradually and ventilation increased. In October some varieties, such as *P. insigne*, begin to form flower stalks with green leaves at the tips which in this period protect the buds. Plants which already have buds should not be allowed to become too dry, but in any case spraying of the leaves should stop. Warmth-loving varieties should still be kept in a moist and warm atmosphere as the period of their quickest growth shortens in winter months, and they require practically no rest from vegetation.

Paphiopedilum godefroyae

If Paphiopedilums are cultivated for cutting purposes, the blossoms should be left to bloom on the plants for about fourteen days and then cut. When left on the plant they survive for about two months.

Paphiopedilums can also be cultivated in the home. Those that thrive in a cold atmosphere grow well near a window, particularly one facing north, while warmth-loving varieties grow well in glazed cabinets provided with artificial heating. Otherwise the conditions governing their cultivation in the home are the same as those applicable for greenhouses.

P. argus (PFITZ.) This plant comes from the Philippine Islands. The leaves can be up to 6 inches (15 centimetres) long, light in colour and spotted. The flower stalk is 14—16 inches (35—40 centimetres) long, and has blossoms up to 4 inches (10 centimetres) across. The calyx is white with green stripes along its length, and the base spotted in blackish-purple. The petals of the blossoms are light purple with black dots, while the labellum is brownish-purple. The orchid blooms in April and May.

P. arthurianum (CROMBLEHOLME.) The leaves of this orchid are dark green with a faint marble pattern and are 1 inch (2·5 centimetres) wide and 8—10 inches (20—25 centimetres) long. The flower stalk is up to 10 inches (25 centimetres) high and bears flowers 4 inches (10 centimetre) across. The whole flower is mauvish-brown in colour with purple veins, and the plant blooms from July up to November.

P. barbatum (PFITZ.) The home of this orchid is Malacca. The leaves are light green in colour with a marble pattern, and are 4—6½ inches (10—16 centimetres) long. The flower stalk is 10 inches (25 centimetres) high and bears one blossom 4 inches (10 centimetres) wide. The calyx is white with red veins, the petals being a greenish-red colour, and the labellum is brownish-purple. Both the flower stalk and the leaves are densely covered in small hairs. The plant flowers from April to August.

P. bellatulum (PFITZ.) Originating from Burma, this plant has short, fleshy, dark green leaves with light spots, the lower parts are moss red. The flower stalk is very short. The blossoms are 2½ inches (6 centimetres) across, pure white in colour with purple spots. The plant flowers in March and April.

P. callosum (PFITZ.) Siam is the home of this orchid which has light green leaves with dark stripes. The flower stalk is 10—12 inches (25—30 centimetres) long with one to two flowers 4 inches (10 centimetres) wide. The calyx is striped in reddish-mauve and the labellum brownish-purple. The plant blooms from March to June.

Paphiopedilum arthurianum

P. curtisii (PFITZ.) The home of this plant is Sumatra. The leaves are elliptic and up to 8 inches (20 centimetres) long, and marble-patterned. The flower stalk is 12 inches (30 centimetres) high bearing blossoms 5 inches (12 centimetres) wide. The calyx is white with carmine veins, and the petals are pendent. Their upper half is brownish-red and their lower pink. The labellum is shiny and brownish-black. This variety blooms in March and April.

P. fairieanum (PFITZ.) This orchid comes from Assam and the leaves are dark green. The flower stalk is 6—8 inches (15—20 centimetres) high and the blossoms 3 inches (8 centimetres) across. The calyx and petals are faintly green in colour with brownish-mauve stripes and the labellum is greenish-red with purple veins. The plant blossoms in June and up to November.

P. godefroyae (PFITZ.) This variety is very small in size and has brownish-green, marble-patterned leaves. The blossoms grow from a short stalk, and are white with dark mauvish-brown spots. The plant blossoms in April and May, and originates from Siam.

P. venustum (PFITZ.) The Himalayas are the home of this orchid which has short leaves, brown on their lower side. The flower stalk is 8 inches (20 centimetres) high. The blossoms are 3 inches (8 centimetres) wide and the calyx widely subovate, white in colour with green veins. This variety blooms in November and December.

P. villosum (PFITZ.) This orchid comes from Burma and has leaves 8—16 inches (20—40 centimetres) long. The flower stalk is 10 inches (25 centimetres) high and the blossoms 6 inches (15 centimetres) wide. The calyx is widely elliptic and olive green in colour with white blotches. The petals and labellum of the flowers are brownish-yellow and the plant blossoms from November to May.

Paphiopedilum venustum

Pescatorea

These epiphytic orchids have long, lanceolate leaves among which individual blossoms appear on short stems. The petals and sepals are branched, blunt and subovate, and the labellum is relatively small and hemispherical. About ten varieties come from western tropical America.

Pescatorea require special care during their cultivation. In the summer months they should be kept in a hot greenhouse and in winter in a moderate one. They can be transplanted when new roots begin to appear, usually in spring, in epiphytic orchid soil mixture with good drainage material. During the vegetation period these orchids require moist, warm, fresh air and shade. When the plants have taken root care must be taken to ensure that they receive adequate moisture, and in hot weather they can be sprayed several times daily.

P. cerina (RCHB. F.) This orchid comes from Costa Rica. The leaves are 8—12 inches (20—30 centimetres) long and light green in colour, always growing in fours to sixes. The centre leaves are longer than the side leaves and the flower stalk is 4 inches (10 centimetres) long. The petals and sepals are elliptic, waxy and yellow in colour. The labellum is small and partly subovate, lemon yellow in colour interwoven with red. The plant flowers in June and July.

P. dayana (RCHB. F.) This plant comes from Colombia. It resembles the previously described variety, but its growth is more abundant. The blossoms are up to 3½ inches (9 centimetres) wide and the petals and sepals are fleshy, elliptic, and creamy white in colour with reddish tips. The labellum is mauve with lighter edges. The plant blossoms from July to September.

P. lehmanni (RCHB. F.) This orchid also originates from Colombia and has leaves 12—16 inches (30—40 centimetres) long. The flower stalk is partly pendent with blossoms 2½—3½ inches (7—9 centimetres) across. The petals and sepals are partly subovate, and are white in colour with wide mauve stripes. The labellum is oval in shape and mauve. This variety flowers from May to November.

Pescatorea cerina

Phaius

This genus comprises semi-terrestrial and, in rare cases, epiphytic orchids with elongated stalks or leaf stems. The flower stalk grows above the leaves and bears luxuriant clusters of flowers. About thirty varieties come from West Africa and southern Asia.

These plants can be successfully cultivated in a warm environment, and should be transplanted at the beginning of their vegetation period in soil suitable for terrestrial orchids. During the period of growth they require extensive watering, moist air and light shade and in winter should be watered rarely and in small amounts. However, if left in an overdry atmosphere they become susceptible to attack from harmful insects. The genus includes some beautiful varieties which together with some of the hybrids are very suitable for cutting.

P. humboltii (RCHB. F.) The home of this variety is Madagascar. It has thick leaf stems which bear two to three leaves, and the upright flower stalk has sparse clusters of seven to ten blossoms about 2 inches (5 centimetres) wide. The petals and sepals are white in colour with pinkish-red stripes, and the labellum red with yellowish-brown spots. The plant flowers in June and July.

P. tankervilliae (BL.) This orchid comes from India and has short, oval leaf stems with four to six narrow, elliptic leaves. The flower stalk is about 32 inches (80 centimetres) long and bears ten to twelve blossoms 4½ inches (12 centimetres) across. The petals and sepals of the flowers are yellowish-brown in colour towards their inside with silvery-white edges. The labellum is widely oval and yellowish-brown. The plant blooms from February to April.

P. wallichii (LDL.) Originating from tropical Asia and Australia, this orchid has short, oval leaf stems with two to three leaves up to 32 inches (80 centimetres) long. The flower stalk grows in an upright manner and bears seven to ten blossoms. The whole flower is light brownish-red, while the labellum is darker on its inside. The plant flowers in December and January and the blossoms survive for more than a month.

Phaius wallichii

Phalaenopsis

The orchids of this genus are epiphytic and have no stems, but short, leaf axils. The leaves are fleshy and non-deciduous. The flower stalk is slender with branched inflorescences. About forty varieties come from Burma, South Vietnam, the Philippines and Indonesia.

The genus *Phalaenopsis* includes a number of exquisitely beautiful hybrids. These plants have very exacting requirements as regards temperature and air humidity, particularly during the vegetation period. A double-glazed greenhouse is suitable for cultivation, in which the necessary temperature can be maintained during even severe frosts. They should be planted in flat bowls, wooden baskets are more suitable for larger varieties. Spring is the best time for transplanting which should be carried out with the greatest care to prevent damage to the roots. If some roots have become attached to the wood, they must be cut carefully. The soil mixture for epiphytic orchids is suitable but with a high concentration of *Sphagnum* which can also be placed on the surface of the soil afterwards. These orchids grow well when hung about 16 inches (40 centimetres) from the glass.

During the vegetation period the orchids require a temperature of about 30°C (86°F), frequent spraying and considerable shade. In summer plants that have taken root can be fertilized with a weak manure solution and if the plants are hung above this solution the roots will grow down to its surface. The ground in the greenhouse should also be kept moist and can be ensured by frequently watering the pathways and walls. In winter up to March, i.e. in the non-vegetation period, watering should be restricted and the temperature lowered to 20°C (68°F). If the summer months are cool, the greenhouse must be heated as the successful cultivation of these orchids depends on a constant temperature.

The fully grown blossoms should be cut when they begin to fade so that they may not weaken the plant. Young plants should be grown in flowerpots placed on tables covered with fresh *Sphagnum.*

Phalaenopsis heideperle

Phalaenopsis can be successfully cultivated in the home only in a glazed window box or glass show-case with artificial heating and lighting. However, it is still essential to maintain the conditions of greenhouse cultivation, namely a temperature of 25—30°C (77—86°F), shade and moisture in summer, and 20°C (68°F) and more light in winter.

P. amabilis (BL.) This orchid comes from Java and Borneo. It has long subovate leaves up to 12 inches (30 centimetres) long, light green in colour. The flower stalk is slender and bears a branched inflorescence with six to fifteen blossoms. The individual blooms are up to 4 inches (10 centimetres) wide and are white in colour with a yellow, red-striped labellum. The plant flowers from October to January.

P. heideperle This plant has hanging, dark green elliptic leaves with a faint marble pattern. The flower stalk is slightly bent and bears eight to ten blooms which are up to 4 inches (10 centimetres) wide, pink in colour with a faint mauvish tint. The labellum is of a darker shade. The plant blooms in spring.

P. schilleriana (RCHB. F.) The home of this plant is the Philippine Islands. The leaves are pendent and elliptic, coloured dark green and streaked transversally in greyish-white. The flower stalk is also pendent, and slightly branched with an abundance of blossoms. The individual flowers are up to 4 inches (10 centimetres) across, and are light pink with a red spotted labellum. This variety blooms from February to May.

P. stuartiana (RCHB. F.) This plant also comes from the Philippines. The leaves are greyish-green and the flowers small, 2 inches (5 centimetres) across. The sepals and half of the petals are white while the other half are a greenish colour with brownish-red spots. The labellum is whitish-yellow with brownish-red spots. The plant flowers from January to March.

Phalaenopsis stuartiana

Phragmipedilum

The orchids comprising this genus are evergreen and closely resemble those of the genus *Paphiopedilum*. The leaves are strap-shaped and light green in colour. The flower stalk bears a number of blooms and the inflorescence is often branched. About twelve varieties are widespread in Colombia, Peru and Brazil.

Phragmipedilums should be grown in a temperature greenhouse, and transplanted when they begin to form new roots. Flowerpots are suitable and terrestrial orchid soil should be used. During the summer months the plants can be watered well, but should receive less water in winter. They should be lightly shaded in summer. These orchids are relatively easy to cultivate and are popular among orchid growers.

P. caudatum (ROLFE.) The home of this orchid is Peru. The leaves are 10—16 inches (25—40 centimetres) long and 1 inch (2·5 centimetres) wide. The flower stalk can be 40 inches (1 metre) long and is entirely covered in down. It bears two to three blossoms whose sepals are striped in brown; the petals are elongated in a tail-like manner, pendent, and yellowish-green in colour. The labellum is long and brownish-green and has a white mouth with red spots. The plant blooms from April to August.

P. longifolium (ROLFE.) This plant comes from Costa Rica. It has pointed leaves 24 inches (60 centimetres) long 1 inch (2·5 centimetres) wide. The flower stalk bears six to ten blooms. The individual blossoms are up to 7 inches (18 centimetres) across and are light green in colour with purple stripes. The labellum is yellowish-green and its front part a lightish brown. The plant blossoms throughout the whole year.

P. sedenii (ROLFE.) Originating from Peru, this orchid has pointed leaves ½ inch (1 centimetre) wide and 10 inches (25 centimetres) long and light green in colour. The flower stalk can be up to 12 inches (30 centimetres) high and bears a number of blooms. The petals and sepals of the flowers are light pink with a whitish tint. This variety also flowers the whole year round.

Phragmipedilum sedenii

Pleione

The orchids are epiphytic types with subovate leaf stems bearing long, elliptic leaves which are shed every year. The blossoms are large and grow singly, resembling those of the genus *Coelogyne*. About fifteen varieties come from the Himalayas.

Orchids of the genus *Pleione* should be cultivated in a shady, cold greenhouse. They can be transplanted when they begin to grow new shoots and roots, as a rule after the blossoming period. A soil mixture comprising two thirds *Sphagnum* and one third *Osmunda* should be used. The orchids should then be watered only in small amounts, and watering increased only if the plants develop brown leaves. In the summer months they require good ventilation. After the leaves have fallen in autumn the plants require a period of complete rest, but as soon as buds begin to appear at the bases of the leaf stems, watering can be recommenced.

Pleione orchids are quite small plants with beautiful flowers, and are particularly suitable for cultivation by amateur growers. They can be grown well in a cold environment in the home, and a room with a window facing north is ideal.

P. formosanum (LDL.) This plant has rounded leaf stems which grow to a height of 1 inch (2·5 centimetres) and bear oval leaves. The blossoms can be 3 inches (8 centimetres) wide and are coloured light pinkish-mauve. The orchid blooms in March when it has no leaves and it is only when the flowers have faded that new leaves form.

P. humilis (DON.) This orchid has subovate leaf stems which narrow towards their tips and grow to a height of 1½—2½ inches (4—6 centimetres). The leaves are elliptic and can be up to 5 inches (13 centimetres) long. The blossoms are 2 inches (5 centimetres) across and white in colour. The wide oval labellum is also white but has a golden-yellow patterned front part, with red-spotted edges. This variety blossoms in November.

P. lagenaria (LDL.) This orchid has bottle-shaped leaf stems with elliptic leaves up to 5 inches (12 centimetres) long. The flower stalk bears only one blossom which is mauvish-pink in colour with a red and yellow-spotted labellum. The plant blossoms in October and November.

P. pogonioides (ROLFE.) This orchid is quite small with a round, somewhat compressed stem 1 inch (2·5 centimetres) high. The leaves are elongated, and blossoms 2½ inches (6 centimetres) wide, reddish-mauve in colour. The labellum is also reddish-mauve with a golden-yellow pattern. The plant blooms in April and May.

Pleione formosanum

Sobralia

The orchids of this genus are high, strong plants most of which have a reed-like appearance. They have wide, clinging leaves and large blossoms resembling those of the genus *Cattleya*. The flowers grow either singly or in sparse clusters, growing from the axils of the leaves. About sixty varieties come from tropical America.

Plants of the genus *Sobralia* should be transplanted in spring after the blossoming period, using soil for terrestrial orchids. At the same time they can also be propagated by division of their clusters. Smaller varieties should be planted in flat bowls and larger ones in wooden tubs and once transplanted, the orchids can be watered less frequently, although sprayed several times a day. When the plants have taken root they can be watered more heavily and frequently. Orchids of this genus should be grown in a temperate greenhouse and during the vegetation period require moisture around the roots as well as a moist atmosphere, and a constant supply of fresh air. These orchids can also be grown successfully in the home, but their blossoms are not suitable for cutting.

S. leucoxantha (RCHB. F.) This orchid comes from Costa Rica and Guatemala. It has a strong, leafy stalk up to 40 inches (1 metre) high, and the blossoms are 5—6 inches (12—15 centimetres) wide, white in colour with an orange labellum with white edges. The plant blooms in July and August.

S. macrantha (LDL.) Originating from Mexico and Guatemala, this plant has leaf stems up to 80 inches (2 metres) high which are densely leafed. The blossoms can be up to 6 inches (15 centimetres) wide, are purplish-mauve in colour with a yellow labellum which has a ragged front part. The plant blossoms from May to August.

S. xantholeuca (RCHB. F.) The home of this orchid is Guatemala. It greatly resembles the *S. leucoxantha* variety, but the blossoms are sulphur-yellow with a golden-yellow labellum. It flowers from June to August.

Sobralia macrantha

Sophronitis

These epiphytic orchids do not grow very high and have small leaf stems with flat leaves. The blossoms are relatively large and grow either singly or in sparse clusters. About seven varieties come from Brazil.

The orchids of this genus should be grown in a cold greenhouse, but they also thrive well in the home. They are very decorative and all varieties grow abundantly. Transplantation can be carried out when the orchids begin to produce new roots and in soil suitable for epiphytic orchids. They can be grown on a piece of cork or branch, or planted in small, flat bowls. In the summer months these orchids require moist, fresh air and a large amount of shade. In winter, on the other hand, they need a great deal of light and a temperature of 10—12°C (50—54°F).

S. cernua (LDL.) This variety comes from Brazil. The leaf stems are up to 1 inch (2·5 centimetres) high, bearing oval leaves with short pointed tips, 1 inch (2·5 centimetres) long. The flower stalk bears two to four blossoms which are salmon pink in colour and 1 inch (2·5 centimetres) wide. The petals are a little wider than the sepals. The plant flowers in December and January.

S. coccinea (LDL.) This plant also comes from Brazil. The leaf stems are 1 inch (2·5 centimetres) high, and the leaves strap-shaped, leathery in texture and 2½ inches (6 centimetres) long. The blossoms grow singly, are 2—3 inches (5—8 centimetres) wide and bright purplish-red in colour. The labellum is orange-yellow with a purplish pattern. The orchid blooms from November to February.

Sophronitis coccinea

Stanhopea

The orchids of this genus are epiphytic with shrivelled leaf stems bearing in most cases one leathery, elliptic leaf. The blossoms of these plants have a wax-like texture, are strongly scented and always grow in hanging clusters. All the varieties of the genus *Stanhopea* come from tropical America.

These orchids should be cultivated in a moderate environment and transplanted early in spring or when they have blossomed, in epiphytic orchid soil. Annual transplantation is not recommended. These orchids should be propagated by division and if the divided parts of the plants are small, they can be planted in flowerpots. Older plants, however, should be set in wooden, suspended baskets, and then left in a warm atmosphere. In summer when they have taken root, they can be hung in a protected place outside, preferably under a tree. Before and during their blossoming period these orchids require extensive watering. This genus can be grown quite easily and is consequently suitable for cultivation by amateurs.

S. devoniensis (LDL.) The flower stalk of this orchid can be up to 4 inches (10 centimetres) high with three strongly-scented blossoms. The petals and sepals are creamy white in colour with red spots. The labellum is white with two purplish-red spots. This variety flowers in July and August.

S. hernandezii (SCHL.) [syn. *S. tigrina* (BATEM.)] This variety has the largest flowers which can be up to 6 inches (15 centimetres) wide. They are yellow in colour with large mauve spots. The labellum is fleshy in appearance. The plant flowers from August to November.

S. oculata (LDL.) This orchid has a flower stalk 6 inches (15 centimetres) long which bears seven blossoms, up to 5½ inches (14 centimetres) wide. The petals and sepals are light green with mauve spots, the labellum is yellow and mauve in front. The plant blooms from July to October.

Stanhopea hernandezii

Thunia

These orchids are terrestrial with leaf stalks bearing regularly placed, lanceolate, greyish-green leaves. The large flowers grow in clusters, with petals and sepals strap-shaped. The labellum is cornet-shaped. About five varieties come from Burma and the Himalayas.

The conditions governing the cultivation of orchids of this genus are similar to those of the genus *Calanthe*. They can be transplanted every year at the beginning of the vegetation period. The plants should be tapped from their pots and old, dead roots and leaf stems removed. Only the stems of the previous year should remain and these planted in small numbers in flowerpots using soil suitable for terrestrial orchids.

When the orchids have been transplanted they should be watered rarely, and more frequently only when the plants begin to grow strongly. Until the new buds appear watering with a weak manure solution proves beneficial. The orchids must be kept in a warm, moist greenhouse, but the leaves need not be sprayed. They can be lightly shaded. The blossoms of the plants appear in the summer months. When the leaves turn yellow and are shed in autumn, watering can be stopped and the plants transferred to an environment with a temperature of 10°C (50°F). *Thunia* have beautiful flowers, but they are not suitable for cutting.

T. alba (RCHB. F.) The home of this variety is the Himalayas. It has a tubular leaf stalk which grows to a height of 16—20 inches (40—50 centimetres) and bears pointed, bluish-green leaves. The blossoms grow in hanging clusters of five to seven, and are white in colour with yellow stripes and a mauve labellum. They are 2 inches (5 centimetres) wide. The plant flowers in July and August.

T. marshalliana (RCHB. F.) This orchid comes from Burma. The leaf stems are up to 40 inches (1 metre) high and end in three blooms 5 inches (12 centimetres) across. The petals and sepals of the blossoms are white as is the labellum which is bent backwards, and has a yellow front part with an orange border. The plant blooms in June and July.

Thunia marshalliana

Trichopilia

This genus comprises epiphytic orchids whose leaf stems have a flat appearance and bear one leathery, dark green leaf. The flower stalks grow from the base of the leaf stems and are pendent with one to five blooms. About fifteen varieties come from tropical America.

Trichopilia orchids should be cultivated in a cold greenhouse and should be transplanted every third year after they have blossomed, in soil with a large concentration of *Osmunda*. During the summer months these orchids require warm, fresh air and shade. Once transplanted, they must be watered carefully, and at the end of September can be gradually prepared for the non-vegetation period. At this time watering should be infrequent and no shade provided. In the winter months a temperature of 10—12°C (50—54°F) is sufficient and they require very little watering. These orchids are very beautiful, low-growing types and particularly suitable for cultivation by amateurs.

T. coccinea (LDL.) This orchid originally came from Costa Rica. It has elongated leaf stems 2—2½ inches (5—7 centimetres) high which bear one elliptic, pointed leaf up to 8 inches (20 centimetres) long. The flower stalk is pendent and bears one to two flowers 5 inches (12 centimetres) wide. The petals and sepals are strap-shaped and greenish-brown in colour. The labellum has wavy edges, its outer surface white and its inner pinkish-red. The plant blooms in April and May.

T. fragrans (LDL.) The home of this plant is Colombia. The leaf stems are narrow and elongated, reaching a height of 4—5 inches (10—13 centimetres). The leaves are elliptic and up to 8 inches (20 centimetres) long. The flower stalk is slightly pendent with two to four strongly scented blossoms 4½ inches (12 centimetres) across. The petals and sepals are long and pointed, and white in colour with a greenish tint. The labellum is widely oval in shape and white with yellow spots. The plant blooms in December and January.

T. tortilis (LDL.) Originating from Guatemala, this orchid has very narrow leaf stems which grow to a height of 1½—3 inches (4—8 centimetres). The leaves are elongated, elliptic, and 7 inches (18 centimetres) long. The flower stalk bears one blossom up to 5 inches (13 centimetres) across. The petals and sepals are light pink in colour with a greenish-yellow border. The labellum is rounded and white with brownish-red veins. This variety blooms in December and January.

Trichopilia tortilis

Vanda

The orchids of this genus come from the monsoon regions of India and the Philippines. They have a strong, upright stalks bearing many leathery leaves from whose axils, clusters, or panicles of medium-sized blossoms grow.

Some varieties are suitable for a warm and others for a cold greenhouse. The plants should always be transplanted after several years. Strong aerial roots growing horizontally must be drawn towards the main stalk while still young, to ensure downward growth. Older roots tend to break on bending. *Vanda* orchids can be transplanted after they have blossomed, when the roots renew their growth, usually in April. With over-tall plants it is advisable to cut the strong tops with well-developed roots, and plant them in flowerpots. The size of the pot can be chosen according to the size of the plants and their roots. The bottom of the pots must be covered with good drainage, and soil suitable for epiphytic orchids used to fill the spaces between the roots.

Once transplanted, the orchids require greater warmth, aerial spraying and during the summer months should be shaded well. In the majority of cases growth of these orchids is from March to August, and from September they can be left in a drier state and exposed to air and sunshine. In autumn and winter the ambient temperature may drop to 14—16°C (57—61°F). Some varieties, such as *V. coerulea*, begin to bloom in December and later types flower from January to February. These varieties should be kept in a warmer atmosphere and watered less frequently. The remaining types flower in March or April. If the non-vegetation and growth periods are observed, *Vanda* orchids blossom annually and stronger plants produce several flower stalks.

V. amesiana (RCHB. F.) This orchid comes from Cambodia. It has a short stalk with thick, fleshy, pointed leaves and a large number of aerial roots. The flower stalk is 16 inches (40 centimetres) long and bears fifteen to twenty blossoms which are white in colour with pink spots, strongly scented, and 1½ inches (4 centimetres) wide. The labellum is trilobate, purple in colour with lighter edges. The plant blooms in December and January.

Vanda coerulea

V. coerulea (GRIFF.) The home of this plant is North India. The stalk bears short, leathery leaves, and can be up to 18 inches (45 centimetres) long with seven to fifteen blossoms each 2½—4 inches (7—10 centimetres) across. The flowers are light blue in colour with a small, dark, bluish-mauve labellum. The orchid blooms in October and November.

V. teres (LDL.) This plant comes from Burma. It has a slender stalk up to 84 inches (2·1 metres) long with narrow, tubular leaves. The flower stalk bears three to five blossoms 3—4 inches (8—10 centimetres) wide. The sepals are almost white in colour and the petals mauvish-pink. The labellum is almost square, with pinkish-red edges and a yellow inner part. The orchid flowers from July to August.

V. tricolor (LDL.) Java is the original home of this orchid which has a strong stalk up to 60 inches (1·5 metres) long with long, strap-shaped leaves. The flower stalk is shorter than the leaves and grows in an upright manner, bearing seven to eight blossoms. These are 2½ inches (7 centimetres) across, strongly scented, and whitish-yellow in colour with brown spots. The labellum is violin-shaped and white, with mauvish-pink sides and purple stripes on its front part. This variety blooms from February to May.

V. tricolor var. *suavis* (RCHB. F.) Java is the home of this orchid which has a 60 inches (1·5 metres) long stalk with long, strap-shaped leaves. It resembles closely *V. tricolor* variety, but has, however, a longer pendent flower stalk with more luxuriant inflorescences. The petals and sepals of the blossoms are white in colour with a number of brownish-mauve spots. The labellum is dark mauve but its front part is lighter. The plant flowers in April and May.

Vanda tricolor var. *suavis*

Zygopetalum

This genus comprises epiphytic and semi-terrestrial orchids. They usually have short, subovate, sometimes somewhat flat leaf stems with two narrow leaves. The flower stalk bears sparse clusters of three to ten blossoms and the labellum forms a 'tree-beard'. About eighteen to twenty varieties come from Brazil, Venezuela and Colombia.

Varieties with developed leaf stems can be grown in a temperate environment, while those with small stems in a warm greenhouse. They should be transplanted in spring when new roots begin to grow, using soil for epiphytic orchids with a large addition of beech leaf. These orchids cannot tolerate over-watered roots and consequently drainage material filling one third of the flowerpot should be provided together with moist, warm fresh air, and light shade. During the non-vegetation period these orchids need be watered only to prevent the leaf stems from drying up.

Z. crinitum (LODD.) This orchid has wide, subovate leaf stems up to 2 inches (5 centimetres) high and bearing two to three leaves 14 inches (35 centimetres) long. The flower stalk is up to 20 inches (50 centimetres) high and bears five to seven blossoms 2½ inches (6—7 centimetres) across. The latter are strongly scented and the petals and sepals are strap-shaped and yellowish-green in colour with purplish-brown streaks. The labellum is white and hairy, with its surface covered with a purple veined pattern. The plant blossoms from October to December.

Z. mackaii (HOOK.) This plant has subovate leaf stems up to 2½ inches (6 centimetres) high, with leaves 12 inches (30 centimetres) long. The flower stalk bears five to seven blooms 2½ inches (6—7 centimetres) across. The petals and sepals are yellowish-green in colour with purplish-brown streaks. The front part of the labellum is ragged with longitudinal bluish-mauve stripes. The plant flowers from November to February. The home of both varieties is Brazil.

Zygopetalum crinitum

INDEX

Ada aurantiaca 28, 29
— *lehmannii* 28
Aerangis articulatum 30
— *citratum* 30, 31
— *modestum* 30
Aerides odoratum 32
— *vandarum* 32, 33
Angraecum eburneum 34, 35
— *sesquipedale* 34
Anguloa clowesii 36, 37
— *ruckeri* 36
Anoectochilus regalis 38, 39
— *setaceus* 38

Bifrenaria atropurpurea 40
— *harrisoniae* 40, 41
Brassavola digbyana 42
— *glauca* 42
— *perrinii* 42, 43
Brassia maculata 44
— *verrucosa* 44, 45
Bulbophyllum barbigerum 46
— *carreyanum* 46, 47
— *lobii* 46

Calanthe veratrifolia 48
— *vestita* 48, 49
Catasetum fimbriatum 50, 51
— *macrocarpum* 50
— *pileatum* 50
Cattleya amethystoglossa 54
— *bowringiana* 56
— *citrina* 53, 56
— *dowiana* 56
— *horace* 55, 56
— *labiata* 58
— *miniscia* 57, 58
— *mossiae* 58
— *percivaliana* 58
— *trianae* 58, 59
Chysis bractescens 60, 61
— *laevis* 60
— *limminghei* 60
Cochlioda densiflora 62, 63
— *rosea* 62
— *sanguinea* 62
Coelogyne asperata 66
— *cristata* 65, 66
— *dayana* 66
— *massangeana* 66, 67
Cymbidium adrian 69, 70
— *giganteum* 70
Cymbidium insigne 70
— *lowianum* 70
— *nicolasianum* 70, 71

Dendrobium chrysanthum 74
— *chrysotoxum* 74
— *crassinode* 76
— *devonianum* 76
— *fimbriatum* 76
— *finlayanum* 73, 76
— *moschatum* 75, 76
— *nobile* 76
— *nobile* var. *sanderianum* 77, 78
— *phalaenopsis* 78, 79
— *pierardii* 78
— *superbiens* 78

Epidendrum prismatocarpum 80
— *stamfordianum* 80
— *vitellinum* 80, 81

Laelia crispa 82
— *gouldiana* 82, 83
— *harpophylla* 84, 85
— *pumila* 84
— *purpurata* 84
Lycaste aromatica 87, 88
— *cruenta* 88
— *skinneri* 88, 89

Masdevallia bella 90
— *caudata* 90
— *chimaera* 90, 91
— *coccinea* 90
Maxillaria grandiflora 92
— *venusta* 92, 93
Miltonia candida 94
— *phalaenopsis* 94
— *spectabilis* 94, 95

Odontoglossum cirrhosum 98
— *citrosmum* 98
— *crispum* 98
— *grande* 97, 98
— *insleayi* 98, 99
Oncidium cavendishianum 100
— *crispum* 100
— *incurvum* 102
— *kramerianum* 102
— *papilio* 102
— *splendidum* 101, 102
— *varicosum* 102, 103
Paphiopedilum argus 108
— *arthurianum* 108, 109
— *barbatum* 108
— *bellatulum* 108
— *callosum* 108
— *curtisii* 110
— *fairieanum* 105, 110
— *godefroyae* 107, 110
— *venustum* 110, 111
— *villosum* 110
Pescatorea cerina 112, 113
— *dayana* 112
— *lehmanni* 112
Phaius humboltii 114
— *tankervilliae* 114
— *wallichii* 114, 115
Phalaenopsis amabilis 118
— *heideperle* 117, 118
— *schilleriana* 118
— *stuartiana* 118, 119
Phragmipedilum caudatum 120
— *longifolium* 120
— *sedenii* 120, 121
Pleione formosanum 122, 123
— *humilis* 122
— *lagenaria* 122
— *pogonioides* 122

Sobralia leucoxantha 124
— *macrantha* 124, 125
— *xantholeuca* 124
Sophronitis cernua 126
— *coccinea* 126, 127
Stanhopea devoniensis 128
— *hernandezii* 128, 129
— *oculata* 128

Thunia alba 130
— *marshalliana* 130, 131
Trichopilia coccinea 132
— *fragrans* 132
— *tortilis* 132, 133

Vanda amesiana 134
— *coerulea* 135, 136
— *teres* 136
— *tricolor* 136
— *tricolor* var. *suavis* 136, 137

Zygopetalum crinitum 138, 139
— *mackaii* 138